The **NICE** *Handbook*

SIMPLE INSTRUCTIONS FOR
Making a Big Difference

Ruth Peterson

Avon, Massachusetts

Published by
Adams Media, a division of F+W Media, Inc.
57 Littlefield Street, Avon, MA 02322. U.S.A.
www.adamsmedia.com

Contains material adapted and abridged from *1,001 Ways to Do Good* by Meera Lester, copyright
© 2008 by F+W Media, Inc., ISBN 10: 1-59869-474-X, ISBN 13: 978-1-59869-474-1.

ISBN 10: 1-4405-7354-9
ISBN 13: 978-1-4405-7354-5
eISBN 10: 1-4405-7355-7
eISBN 13: 978-1-4405-7355-2

Printed in the United States of America.

10 9 8 7 6 5 4 3 2 1

*This book is available at quantity discounts for bulk purchases.
For information, please call 1-800-289-0963.*

NICE

nīs • adjective
kind, pleasing, agreeable, virtuous, respectable

Source: *Merriam-Webster Dictionary*

Fed up with all the depressing stories on the news? Tired of all the negativity you hear from your friends? Annoyed that the guy who works in your office didn't hold the elevator door/ate the last jelly doughnut/didn't tip the delivery guy? Wish things were just a little more . . . nice?

Whether you just want to put a smile on a loved one's face or help someone out in a big way, *The Nice Handbook* shows you how to add some nice into your day—and into the days of the people around you! Featuring more than 500 deeds that help you spread that warm and fuzzy feeling, this book will even encourage the biggest curmudgeon to have a change of heart. Here, you'll find fun and simple ways to let your inner kindness show, including:

- Mowing your neighbor's yard
- Preparing a hot drink for your letter carrier in the winter
- Teaching a local arts and crafts class
- Doing laundry for a new mom in your community
- Writing a thank-you note to a helpful coworker
- Giving up your window seat to another passenger

And the generosity doesn't stop there—by simply being nice, you'll jumpstart a ripple effect of good deeds. You'll find that when you go out of your way to brighten someone else's day, you'll also inspire friends, family, and even strangers to do nice things for others in their lives. For example, maybe you decide to donate books to a local elementary school. Someone sees you do this good deed and, feeling motivated, volunteers to read to children at the library, which inspires someone else to coach the boys' soccer team. All of a sudden, the world is a better place just because you went out of your way to be nice.

So flip through the pages and pick out some ways to brighten someone's day. And remember, when you smile, the whole world smiles back. Why wouldn't you want that good karma coming your way?

Adopt an acre of vital wetlands. The African wetlands are in danger. Your support can help save these important migration areas. Check out *www.awf.org* to learn more about this type of geographical area and what you can do to save it.

Help those impacted by natural disasters. Donate to the latest natural disaster–relief fund via the American Red Cross (*www.redcross.org*). Your donation—be it time, goods, or money—will be of great help to the thousands of families whose lives have been turned upside down by a natural disaster.

Make a treat to cheer up a gloomy Monday. It could be a healthy snack, an old Midwestern pineapple upside-down cake, or a special little box of Scottish shortbread to savor with a hot cup of tea. Any little treat on a Monday will usually brighten the mood in the office and start the workweek off right.

Drive an elderly neighbor to a doctor's appointment. Getting to and from appointments may seem mundane to healthy, young, energetic individuals, but it can be a major headache for an elderly person without easy and accessible transportation.

Drop by a friend's house with iced coffee.

Help set up a school's computer lab. Contact your local school and put your technological know-how to use. Most schools do not have an in-house IT professional, so by volunteering you're helping children's education and saving the school system money.

Recycle used plastic grocery store bags. If you forget to bring your reusable bag with you to the grocery store, don't feel too bad taking plastic as long as you bring it back to the store's bag recycling box later!

Show a kid how to ride a bicycle. Bike riding is a wonderful activity for children, which gets them out in the fresh air. However, it can be a scary thing to learn how to do. Help your child or a neighborhood child learn how to pedal, steer, and brake her bike without her training wheels. Make sure she's wearing the proper helmet and pads before you do.

Clean up your language. It's easy to fall into the habit of using bad English, slang, and profanity. Make an effort to speak better English. Excellent language skills improve your personal image wherever you go in the world, and you will be setting a good example for others.

Start a community garden. Get members of your neighborhood and community to come together for this beautifying and eco-friendly endeavor. It creates green space in cities and gives gardeners a way to share the land, their skills, and their bounty with their community.

Send a bouquet on a random day.

Swap supplies. Trade art materials with fellow artists, books with book lovers and writers, kitchen tools with friends who cook, and gardening seed and equipment with fellow gardeners. Why buy when you can swap?

Orchestrate a spa day for your favorite girlfriends. Have it at your house. Arrange to have a manicurist, a massage therapist, and a hair and makeup expert come and teach you how to correctly do your nails, or your hair and makeup, and enjoy a massage.

Place a love note somewhere hidden. Stick it inside his or her lunch pail, wallet, or jacket pocket. It is sure to inspire a smile when he or she unexpectedly discovers it.

Adopt a special needs child. These little ones are most in need of loving families. The children are located in various countries of the world. Look into organizations such as Wide Horizons for Children or Brittany's Hope (a foundation that helps place such children). Some organizations have picture galleries and descriptions of children who are waiting. For more information on the two just mentioned, see *www.whfc.org* and *www.brittanyshope.org*.

Give someone a gift— just because.

Give a card to celebrate a child's achievement. Cards are not just for birthdays. Find a blank card or make a card and inscribe it with a message celebrating a child's athletic achievement, good grades, or specific accomplishment. Kids love getting their own cards.

Become a global pen pal. Through the Internet, you can bring a little joy into the life of a shut-in, befriend others, start a campaign for a favorite cause, or just learn about another person's culture through e-mails.

Purchase beauty products that do not test on animals. Make sure when you're buying makeup, soap, shampoo, and other toiletries that you check to make sure that the company does not test on animals. This is often stated on the back of the container, or you can visit the company's website.

Volunteer at your child's school. Offer to drive on a field trip, set up for a holiday party, work in the library, or serve as a teacher's aide. There are plenty of small things parents can do that can be a big help to teachers. Volunteer even if you don't have a child in school.

Opt for a ceramic mug rather than a Styrofoam cup. Bring a mug from home to the office so the next time you go for a cup of coffee or tea, you can use a reusable cup rather than waste a disposable one. Talk to your manager about seeing if the company will purchase a new mug for everyone in the building so Styrofoam will be obsolete in your office.

Give gifts to a needy family during the winter holidays. Rather than exchanging gifts between family members, organize a gift drive to help a needy family outside the United States. You can either collect the actual gifts, or ask that family members donate the amount of money they would have spent on purchasing family gifts.

Support literacy programs. Teach a child or an illiterate person to read. It will change their lives for the better and you'll be earning some good karma. Check out *http://lincs.ed.gov* for more information.

Give sponsorship to an orphaned chimpanzee. Visit *www .ida-africa.org* to sponsor an orphaned chimpanzee. This makes a great alternative gift at the holidays!

Play a part in protecting the oceans' reefs. Pledge money to save a specific area of these underwater wonders and receive a deed to the reef section you are personally protecting. Visit *www.savenature.org* to purchase your patch.

Donate anonymously to an area museum.

Do laundry for a new mom. If a friend has recently had a baby, offer to wash, dry, and fold her clothes. She could use the time to nap when the baby is sleeping, and she may still be less than one hundred percent after giving birth.

Promote Native American cultural literacy. If keeping alive the cultural traditions of America's indigenous people is important to you, take some action, however small, to bring about the goal desired by you or your group for increasing knowledge about Native American traditions.

Teach a child to swim. If spending time in the water is fun for the child, he will enjoy trying new things, like diving, racing, or a variety of water sports. Swimming is experiential knowledge, so once he learns how to do it, he'll never forget. And if he becomes a decent swimmer, he may one day save his own life or perhaps the life of another.

Rally against genetically altered food. If your passion is a food supply that is all natural and pesticide-free, as well as free from genetic manipulation, find and support a group that fights for the cause.

Buy a goat for a Third World family. This small gesture will help the family move out of poverty. The family will have goat's milk to drink and will be able to sell the extra. Goat manure will enrich the soil, enabling the family to grow a crop that can be sold for money. See *www.goodgifts.org* or *www.heifer.org*.

Be a volunteer Boy Scout or Girl Scout leader. Not only will you be working with young people, teaching important skills in a fun way, but you will also be serving as an example of a volunteer who believes in good citizenship.

Promote the preservation of women's art. Support female cultural heritage by backing female endeavors in art, music, literature, and dance. Increasingly, universities and colleges (in the United States and elsewhere in the world) are including women's studies in their programs. The more you support these endeavors, the more chances a young girl has at attaining her artistic dreams.

Recycle your coffee grounds. Keep an empty coffee can handy in your kitchen to collect the grounds after brewing. You can either deposit them in your compost or use them as fertilizer in your garden.

Donate your videotapes, books, and DVDs to a local library. The library can sell them during a fundraising event to generate funds to purchase new library materials or equipment. Strong school library programs increase learning, yet school libraries as well as city and county libraries are struggling. Spending on new acquisitions of books and other items has been slashed as funding sources have dried up. Your donation is desperately needed. See *www.ala.org/ advocacy/libfunding/fed*.

Babysit for a single parent or family in need for free. Childcare costs can be a huge burden and can prevent single parents from earning their much-needed maximum potential income. If you can offer to help for a couple of hours here and there, you'll be doing a great service.

Donate your tools. Help a village lift itself out of poverty through micro-enterprise. Check out *www.sustainable village.com* and see how you can help them succeed.

Become a conservation volunteer. Work with the park and recreation departments of local communities to restore natural habitats while learning about ecology, botany, local wildlife, and public land management issues. Build a path, do some dry stone walling, plant some trees and bushes, or do something else that is good for preserving or creating green spaces in your community.

Control pests naturally, rather than with chemicals. Take a class on how to control pests in your yard and garden using natural means and companion plantings rather than using products that poison or otherwise harm the earth. Find information on sustainable crops, use of manure, and companion planting at *www.attra.org/attra-pub/complant.html.*

Start an oral history project about your community. Get students at a local school to interview senior citizens. A collection of the personal histories of seniors and their memories of the community and world can be housed in a local library or public center.

Protect endangered species of birds. Do something to help ensure that the Whooping Crane, the Mexican Spotted Owl, the Ivory-Billed Woodpecker, and the Puerto Rican Parrot, along with hundreds of other birds on the endangered species watch list, do not go extinct. Find out more at *http://web4.audubon.org/bird/iba.*

Plan a holiday party for your neighbors. Initiate setting up the logistics of a holiday party this December on your street. Get at least two other neighbors to help you. Plan a traveling dinner: appetizers at one house, salad and soup at the next, the entrée at the third house, and desserts at the fourth.

Sponsor an acre of rain forest. Make a forty-dollar donation in the name of someone for whom you would otherwise purchase a birthday gift or anniversary present. See *www.rainforestconcern.org*.

Teach a budding artist a new craft. Show them how to knit a sweater, mold clay on a potter's wheel, hammer together a birdhouse, crochet a blanket, etch a piece of glass, embroider a pillowcase, apply mosaic to a ceramic picture frame, or sew a traditional quilt.

Make a donation to your local parks department. Parks and public places are for all to share—your contribution will help them to become better places for everyone in your community to enjoy.

Donate an old car to benefit children. Through Agape's Kars for Kids program you can put your used car to good use. Agape is a not-for-profit organization in Nashville, Tennessee, with a mission to help children who have been abused or neglected or are in foster care. You get a tax credit for your donation. For more information see *www.kars4kids.org*.

Give a clean glass of water. The money from giving up a cup of gourmet latte every day for one week could buy a micro filter to ensure a developing nation's school drinking water is safe. Visit *www.unicefusa.org* to donate toward the cause of safe drinking water.

Teach a child how to tie her shoelaces. If you see a child running around with her shoes untied, ask her if she wants you to help tie them. Demonstrate how to tie the laces with one shoe, and then let her practice on her other shoe.

Call an elderly relative just to say hello.

Build your vocabulary and end hunger—at the same time. Visit *www.freerice.com* and play a simple (but addictive) vocabulary game. For every word you get right, the organization donates twenty grains of rice through the UN World Food Program.

Donate to the Elephant Sanctuary. Elephants come from all over the world to rest at this sanctuary in Tennessee. By visiting the website at *www.elephants.com* you can even watch them on the live webcam!

Do your part to clean our shores. Join the worldwide effort to clean up trash lying along the shorelines of the world's oceans, rivers, and lakes. For more information, see *www .oceanconservancy.org*.

Plant bulbs around your house. With the help of your family, plant them in front of your house, next to the ugly parking strip in front, or along the front entrance walkway. Your neighbors will be looking out their windows in the spring to enjoy the flowers you planted and will appreciate your taking the time and effort to create such a display.

Send a postcard to a child you know. Next time you travel, jot off a quick hello and let him know about the place you're visiting. Write a simple message crafted for his reading level. Include little drawings or colorful stickers. Children love getting mail addressed to them.

Walk your neighbor's dog. If your neighbor doesn't have time to join you on your walk, just take his pet. If you don't have a local dog park, take the dog on leash for a brisk walk through the city. Enjoy the day and the sights of the neighborhoods.

Defend the earth. Become a member of the Natural Resources Defense Council (NRDC) and join the effort to fight to save the nation's wildlife and wild places. If your passion is protecting the environment, check out the NRDC website at *www.nrdc.org*.

Empower women around the world. Make a donation to the Women's Learning Partnership. This organization helps women in developing countries network and gain the leadership skills they need to transform themselves, their families, and their societies. Visit its website at *www .learningpartnership.org* to see how you can help.

Plant a tree. Urban forests help improve air quality. Trees absorb carbon dioxide and release oxygen into the atmosphere. One tree gives enough oxygen back through photosynthesis to support two human beings. To discover other interesting facts about trees, go to *www.coloradotrees.org/benefits.htm*; to plant a tree in memory of a loved one, visit *www.arborday.org*.

Create an arts program for underprivileged children. Form a group committed to teaching about the arts and reach out to your community. Maybe your strength lies in the area of finance, public relations, art education, or networking. Whatever it is, use your expertise to help develop and launch the program.

Recycle old Christmas cards. Cut out pieces and use them as gift tags. Or turn them into new cards or collage materials for kids.

Sign up to be a bone marrow donor. This decision could help save someone else's life. On an average day, doctors search the database in order to match 6,000 men, women, and children with potential donors. Learn how you can be a part of this donor database at *www.marrow.org*.

Help volunteers volunteer. Make a donation to Volunteer-Match (*www.volunteermatch.org*), which helps people find the perfect place to volunteer their time and do their own good.

Become a Red Cross volunteer. The Red Cross is perhaps the best-known relief organization offering medical and other types of help in times of disaster. See *www.redcross.org* for more information.

Use sand instead of corrosive salt. Keep two milk cartons filled with sand in the trunk of your car. Next time your tires are spinning on snow or ice, pour the sand under them for traction.

Support local farms. Local and family farms are quickly becoming a thing of the past. Support them by buying locally grown produce and by donating to Farm Aid (*www .farmaid.org*).

Leave your estate to a preservation organization. Groups such as the Conservation Foundation (*www.theconservation foundation.org*) accept donated estates for land and watershed preservation. Land endowments preserve natural resources and ensure that future generations will have parks and beautiful places on the earth to enjoy.

Fight hate. Help the Southern Poverty
Law Center teach tolerance and seek
justice for victims of hate crimes. To
learn how you can help and become
involved in the movement, go to *www
.splcenter.org*.

Shovel the snow from your neighbor's steps. Shoveling snow can be a very arduous task. Help out your neighbors who might need an extra hand. Offer to shovel their steps, driveway, and walkway, and take their "thank you" as your only compensation.

Save the polar bear. Considered the world's largest terrestrial carnivore, the polar bear is in danger of becoming extinct by the end of this century because of climate changes affecting its frozen habitat. Do your part to save these arctic animals. Learn more at *www.worldwildlife.org/polarbears*.

Unplug electrical items not in use. Some cell phone chargers, for example, continue to use electrical current even after a cell phone has been removed from them.

Choose the fish you eat carefully. Don't buy shark, Chilean sea bass, North Atlantic halibut, Atlantic cod and salmon, orange roughy, or tuna because their populations have been depleted due to overfishing or practices considered to be harmful to the environment. Check out *www.fishonline.org/advice/avoid*. Do eat other types of fish, like mackerel and trout, because it is good for your heart health and brain.

Support the National Endowment for the Arts. It is a federally funded arts program that promotes excellence in the arts. It also funds arts programs in areas such as inner cities, rural places, and military bases—in short, bringing the arts to all fifty states to enrich the lives of all of us. Visit *www.nea.gov* for more information.

Go batty. Buy a bat house, adopt a bat, or make a donation to Bat Conservation International. Bats devour garden pests, and their guano is a natural fertilizer. To make a donation, visit *www.supportbats.org/donate*.

Help stop child hunger. Children living in Third World countries do not get enough to eat and go without clean drinking water. Create good karma by making a little sacrifice in your lifetime to ensure that a child does not have to endure hunger for another day. Donate a week's worth of money you would spend on going out to eat to *www .feedthechildren.org.*

Propagate and share your plants. Give your plants' and flowers' "offspring" to local groups and neighbors interested in beautifying your neighborhood or community. You will enjoy seeing your plants throughout your community.

Spend time doing puzzles and playing card games. Gather the family together for an afternoon of unplugged fun. The emphasis is on the quality of time spent together, not the cost of the entertainment.

Let your employees know they're appreciated. Make sure your workers know they are wanted with congratulatory e-mails when they achieve their goals, or just a verbal acknowledgement when they've had a great week. People are less likely to switch jobs if they feel they are making a contribution that is appreciated.

Check in regularly on elderly relatives or neighbors. The heat wave of 2003, one of the hottest summers Europe had ever experienced, and the death toll of 14,802 mostly elderly people who died in France should be a lesson for all us. Not only must we safeguard the safety of our aged relatives and neighbors, we must prepare ourselves for the future heat waves that scientists and climatologists predict will rise in the coming years.

Organize an Open Studios event. If you are an art lover and know struggling artists in your community, arrange for other art enthusiasts to visit the studios or homes of local artists and purchase artwork. Everyone benefits.

Reduce CO_2 emissions. With global warming such a hot topic these days, it's easy to learn ways to decrease the size of your carbon footprint. Start with small things like bringing reusable bags with you to the grocery store. Making changes little by little will make a large impact on the health of the environment. For more tips visit *www.planetark.com*.

Donate to the World Wildlife Federation. When you give money to this all-important cause you'll be helping endangered species worldwide. With more and more species being added to the endangered list every year, the animals need your help now more than ever. Visit *www.wwf.org* for more information.

Open up your home to a college student. Offer an empty room in your house to a college student who must live off campus. Although that young person will be busy with studies and perhaps gone a lot to attend classes, he or she may enrich your life in ways you cannot imagine, especially if from a different country and culture.

Collect new toys for homeless shelters. Call on friends and family to donate toys after first calling a local shelter to find out its needs. Collect, wrap, and donate the toys for Christmas to the shelter's children.

Buy several chickens for a family. Instead of donating cash, which disappears quickly, why not donate an animal or two? A family can enjoy—and share—the eggs from the chickens that they raise for many years. Part of Heifer International's mission is to have the family pass along the offspring from their animals, creating a community of giving (*www.heifer.org*).

Donate to keep the planet diverse. Support the work of the International Union for the Conservation of Nature and Natural Resources (IUCN). The organization strives to conserve and preserve the earth's diversity of nature. See *www.IUCN.org*.

Go solar. Consider making your house solar; you'll save money on electricity and do the earth a favor at the same time. Visit *www.gosolar.com* for more information.

Aid in the efforts to curb climate change. Join the monumental endeavor to help scientists predict climate change. It is just one way shared computing power is working. For more information, see *www.climateprediction.net*.

Bring home little souvenirs. When you return home from vacation, give your old maps, foreign coins, subway tickets, extra postcards, and other travel paraphernalia to a child or grandchild. Kids go crazy over such "treasures." Don't be surprised if the items show up at school the next time there is a "show and tell" scheduled.

Help protect the whales. Though whaling is illegal, it is still common practice in some areas of the world. Organizations like the Sea Shepherd Conservation Society are working to shut down this inhumane practice. For more information, visit *www.seashepherd.org*.

Make a loan to an entrepreneur across the globe to help them create better lives for themselves and their families. Kiva (*www.kiva.org*) works with microfinance institutions on five continents to provide loans to people without access to traditional banking systems. For as little as $25, you can help give someone an opportunity to transform their business and their life.

Grab a friend and learn to dance. It's good for your heart and your friend's, too. You both get a healthy workout and have some fun. Better still, you are supporting each other's goals of staying healthy.

Pamper your pooch. Give him homemade, dog-healthy biscuits. These extra-effort treats will show your pet how much you care—and are healthier alternatives to the processed variety. Find a recipe at *www.gourmetsleuth.com*.

Get children out of the fields. Stop the forced labor of children in the agriculture industries of the world. According to Human Rights Watch, more than sixty-nine percent of the 218 million children doing child labor are working in agriculture. See *http://hrw.org/*.

Leave anonymous May Day flowers. Every May first is May Day, and tradition dictates that you leave someone flowers to brighten up their day. This is a great way to make someone smile.

Invite the new hire out to lunch. Starting a new job is hard. One of the reasons is that you don't know the people with whom you work. Help the new person in your office out and invite him to lunch.

Make it a point to remember people's names. It's important to establish a good rapport with business contacts, and a great way to do that is by first recalling their names. People who remember other people's names are often deemed respectful and caring. Associate his or her name with one of his or her physical features to help you remember.

Return elderly neighbors' empty garbage cans. For elderly people, going outside in inclement weather requires special effort. When the sidewalks are wet or covered in snow and ice, the elderly person risks a dangerous fall. Your act of kindness eliminates that risk.

Adopt an endangered species. Organizations are making it fun to donate by letting you adopt an endangered species; often they'll tell you fun facts about your species, like where their habitat is and how your donation will help to keep them off of the endangered list.

Be a mentor to one or more students. Whether they are attending primary school, middle school, or high school, they could benefit greatly from having an older, responsible person guiding them. This may be especially true of children living in single-parent households.

Celebrate Earth Day. April 22 is when the world's attention is focused on making our planet a healthier place for all to live. Take advantage of all the attention. Organize a massive cleanup in conjunction with the holiday. Visit the day's official website—*www.earthday.org*—so you can coordinate your efforts with others across the globe.

Volunteer your skills to Care 2 Make a Difference. This organization has joined in partnership with the Wildlife Conservation Society and also the Nature Conservancy to do good for specific environmental causes. Visit *www.care2 .com* for volunteer opportunities.

End the needless suffering of animals. Become a member of the Animal Welfare Institute. Your membership fee will help the organization stop a number of unnecessary acts of animal cruelty. Sign up today at *www.awionline.org*.

Sponsor a woman. The organization Women for Women (*www.womenfor women.org*) helps women in war-ravaged countries such as Afghanistan and Rwanda to rebuild their lives. Visit the site to learn about sponsorship, volunteering, and getting involved. You can also send a message of support or shop the bazaar.

Send a child to summer music camp. If you know of a child who loves music but can't afford an instrument or can't afford to go to summer camp, help any way you can. You might contact your local Kiwanis Club or Optimist organization; both of these community service groups do good things for children.

Make your shopping count. Rather than just acquiring stuff, shop and give to charity at the same time. Purchase items in the "hunger site store," "child health site store," "literacy site store," "rainforest site store," and "animal rescue site store." See *www.greatergood.com* for more information.

Help a child with a math problem. Encourage and direct her toward the solution, but don't give her the answer. Use coins or blocks to help her understand the problem. Allow her to discover the solution on her own.

Motivate a friend. Everyone needs a little push now and then to do something. Perhaps she wants to lose weight or learn how to deep-sea dive, dance the Argentine tango, cook a chocolate soufflé, or speak Greek. Urge her to go for it! You might even want to join in. It'll do you both some good.

Recycle using Freecycle.com. If there isn't one where you live, start a Freecycle branch. The Freecycle network is a virtual organization of and for people who wish to recycle rather than throw stuff into landfills. Find items you need and get them free, or post items that you want to give away at *www.freecycle.com*.

Take a volunteer vacation. Want to go abroad but don't want to spend your days fighting through crowds of tourists or lying idle on a beach? Consider taking a volunteer vacation where you can do good while seeing new sights. Organizations such as Global Volunteers (*www.globalvolunteers.com*) and International Volunteer Programs Association (*www.volunteerinternational.org*) can help you plan your trip.

Adopt a section of a highway. Keep it clean and beautiful. Organize a group to help you pick up trash along your designated section of the road. It goes a long way toward keeping America beautiful.

Volunteer with National Children's Coalition. This organization helps at-risk kids who are runaways, abused, or alcohol or chemically addicted. Help where others have given up. For more information, see *www.child.net*.

Use handkerchiefs instead of tissues. It cuts down on paper waste. Find pretty handkerchiefs at thrift stores and secondhand shops or make them from white cotton, cut into squares and hemmed. Decorate with embroidery or stamped art.

Prevent pesticide-related Parkinson's. Use natural pesticides. Find nontoxic alternatives to getting rid of pests in your house. At least one study (done by Emory University in 2002) linked pesticide use in the home with an increase risk of getting Parkinson's disease. Visit *www.cdcg.org* for ideas on organic household pest protection.

Stop the raping of women in the Democratic Republic of Congo. Sexual assaults against women in the D.R.C. has reached an intolerable high. Support the Stop Raping Our Greatest Resource campaign by writing a letter to the president of the D.R.C. Go to the organization's website (*www .stoprapeindrc.org*) for more information.

Leave an encouraging note. If you notice someone in your office is having a particularly bad day, stick a Post-it on her desk with an encouraging message. She will appreciate the kind words.

Help a young family off the plane. Parents traveling with small children have plenty to carry—babies, diaper bags, toys, and a stroller. They were allowed to board first, but the same is not true for when the plane lands and they have to disembark. If you are seated near them, do what you can to help them get off.

Rescue a stuck cat. If you notice a cat trapped up a tree or telephone pole and can get to it without risking your own safety, help it down. Otherwise, call the fire department, local humane society, or other animal rescue organization. If they can't do the rescue, they can help you find someone who can.

Help stop underage drinking. Drunk driving takes the lives of young people every day. Learn more at the website for Mothers against Drunk Driving: *www.madd.org*.

Give your old sewing machine to a local school. When you are ready to buy a newer model, donate your old machine. A student in an art or fashion design program without the means to afford a machine might be able to use it.

Help a war orphan. Visit *www.warchild
.org* and learn about the atrocities inflicted
on millions of children daily as they face
the horrors of war. Make a donation to the
organization on its website and help make
a difference in these children's lives.

Return programs before leaving exhibits. When leaving a cultural event or museum, tuck the catalog back into its slot for others to use rather than taking it home to toss into the recycling bin.

Deliver some homemade lemonade. When a friend receives some bad news, take a pitcher and two glasses to her house, sit down with her, and enjoy a glass together. Sip and be silent while she talks or cries. You are with her to show love and support.

Hold a yard sale. Why sell old junk just to buy new junk? Advertise your yard sale as "all proceeds benefit orphans displaced by the tsunami." That way you'll get rid of your junk *and* make a difference in the world at the same time. Plus, people are less likely to haggle over prices if they know that their money is going to support a worthy cause!

Help a neighbor with a home improvement project. Next time you see a neighbor beginning a project, offer a helping hand. Home accidents account for roughly over 70,000 injuries every year. You can steady a ladder, hand him a tool, or hold something in place.

Stop the exploitation of women and children. Join the effort to stop the world's illicit sex trade. While most countries have this horrific problem, it seems to be exponentially worse in some places than others. Local, regional, and international demand for pornographic images and sexual tourism programs raises serious concerns because it fuels the trafficking of children for sexual exploitation. For more information, see *www.ecpat.net*.

Watch a pet while its owner's on vacation. Whether the pet is an iguana or a horse, take the responsibility seriously and care for the animal exactly as you are instructed. Make certain you have phone numbers and know how to deal with any emergencies that may arise.

Help a coworker succeed. By helping others get ahead in their career, you increase your chances for success as well. Besides, it's good karma for you. We all need a champion in our corner. Be a champion for someone else. When you climb up the career ladder, pull someone up behind you.

Give fair trade presents. Next time you need a birthday, holiday, or "just because" present, skip the obvious and head for a store where you'll find unique items that also do good internationally. At stores like Ten Thousand Villages (*www.tenthousandvillages.com*) and SERRVE (*www.serrv .org*) you'll find lots of fair trade goodies that will make the perfect gift.

Donate a wheelchair to someone in a developing country. Through the Free Wheelchair Mission (*www.freewheel chairmission.org*) you can help provide a wheelchair to someone in desperate need.

Make a contribution to an entrepreneur. If you want to make a donation and know that it's making a very specific difference, look into an organization like the Foundation for International Community Assistance (FINCA, at *www .villagebanking.org*). These companies allow you to make a donation to an entrepreneur in the developing world and learn the specific use of the money.

Become an international aid worker. See the risk in doing nothing and choose an unconventional lifestyle. Be fore-warned, however, that leaving your cubicle to accompany a convoy through a conflict zone or to distribute food and wa-ter in a refugee camp can be hazardous to your health. For some, the value of what they are doing outweighs the risks associated with the work.

Share your home office equipment. Allow a friend to use your fax machine in your home office if he doesn't otherwise have access to such equipment. It's likely your fax equip-ment isn't in use all day, and giving your friend access will save him the time and expense of going to a copy center.

Empower people to make change in their community. Take inspiration from LifeWind, an organization that works in rural villages to help local leaders address their community's problems of poverty and disease by looking at the root. For information visit *www.lifewind.org*.

Set up a fundraising website. You don't need to be doing a specific walk or event to have a fundraising website. Check out the site started by Kevin Bacon, *www.sixdegrees.org*, for more information. On this site you can compete with other charities to see who can raise the most funds.

Recycle nonrecyclable materials. Companies like Terra-Cycle (*www.terracycle.net*) are taking packaging materials from products like energy bars and drink pouches and making them into new products, from tote bags to homework folders. You can mail in your used materials or drop them off at a local center.

Organize a day of silence. The Day of Silence initiative was started to end harassment of LGBT youth, but the style of action can be used to draw attention to other causes as well.

Organize a neighborhood beautification project. Try to get everyone involved. Whether it is decorating for the holidays or planting a rose bush in every yard for a summer garden party, the point is to get everyone involved in meeting each other and working together for the greater good of the neighborhood.

Get in shape for a good cause. Earn money for medical research teams and exercise at the same time by participating in a charity walk. Join forces with the Leukemia Foundation for a Cure or the Fight Against Breast Cancer or the American Heart Association, and walk to raise money for medical research.

Report on local business's greenness. Websites are popping up where you can rate how green a business is and recommend an eco-friendly business to others. Check out *www .izzitgreen.com* for more information.

Stop using pesticides. These chemical treatments can harm the planet and run off into water supplies. Find organic solutions to deter crop infestation, such as companion planting. Use damp newspapers placed on the ground at night in the garden to attract slugs. Then, the next morning, throw away the papers.

Attend a rally. It's hard to ignore thousands of people all gathered together for the same cause. Even if you can't make it to the nation's capital to voice your opinion, rallies are held nationally. Can't find one for your cause? Start one yourself by hanging fliers and posting online.

Fight against turning children into soldiers. The following countries have either abducted or recruited children for warfare and armed conflict: Angola, Burma, Burundi, Colombia, the Democratic Republic of Congo, Lebanon, Liberia, Nepal, Sierra Leone, Sri Lanka, Sudan, and Uganda. Find out what you can do at *www.hrw.org*.

Contribute to a First Response Backpack.
The packs are distributed to soldiers
wounded on the battlefield. There are
no longer MASH units to offer military
medical assistance in the arena of combat.
The wounded are transported to military
hospitals, often without so much as a
toothbrush or change of clothes. The
backpack contains personal items, along
with a phone card so the soldier can
contact family. See *www.soldierangels.org*
for more information.

Click to Give™ free food. Simply visit *www.thehungersite.com* and click on its homepage—and you've donated one cup of food to the world's hungry. Simple as that.

Let go of the need to hold on to the past. You cannot undo what has been done. It's history. Embrace the present and dream of tomorrow.

Offer financial support for refugees. Migrants often seek asylum for reasons of persecution or poverty. If life becomes untenable in their native land, they are forced to move. Often rape, torture, or the lack of economic sources to sustain them leaves them traumatized and destitute. Donate to the cause at *www.amnestyusa.org*.

Be tolerant of family members' lifestyle choices. Respect the rights of your loved ones to follow paths that you may not agree with but that they have chosen. Keep your mouth shut, don't judge them—just remain firm in your support and love.

Join the One Million Signatures Campaign. This organization helps Iranian women who are attempting to gain equal rights through reforming laws in Iran. Visit them online at *www.we-change.org/english.*

Reduce the noise in your office. Cut down on yelling or talking loudly, playing music too loudly, or creating a commotion as you walk down the hallway. According to the Canadian Safety Council's website, problem solving will improve and stress will go down. So do yourself and your coworkers a favor and reduce the noise to improve your productivity.

Help a mentally ill neighbor clean her house. A clutter problem may be the result of a bipolar condition or obsessive-compulsive disorder. Enable her to get her disorganized and cluttered home back under control through a little organization. Help her utilize shelving on walls to get stuff off the floors. Hide clutter in decorative boxes or baskets. Built-in seating areas under windows and drawers under beds can hold a lot of stuff and keep it out of sight until it is needed.

Plan a nature hike with your children. Point out pretty stones, wildlife, flowers, and other things along the way. Children love such walks and will especially enjoy it because you are with them.

Play matchmaker. Have a party and invite two people you know would hit it off. Introduce them at the party and see what happens. Who knows . . . they may spend the rest of their married life thanking you.

Be mindful of your souvenirs. Travel to other lands to learn about other cultures, but be respectful to the local people and honorable in your dealings. Do not purchase items such as cultural treasures (where removal is prohibited), banned resources, or extinct or endangered species.

Donate to Roots of Peace. Once the fighting is over, the danger is not necessarily over. There are still dangerous landmines in several countries, years after the fighting has stopped. To learn about transforming this land, visit *www .rootsofpeace.org*.

Perform music for retirement home residents. The center's residents will love it, and you'll feel good about sharing your talent to lighten the heart of someone else.

Become a human rights activist. Take a

stand and let your government know that

you do not want terrorism to be used as

an excuse to violate human rights—yours

or anyone else's. Go to *www.amnesty.org*

and pledge your support.

Join in the fight to ban cluster bombs. Like landmines, cluster bombs kill indiscriminately. And like landmines, they sometimes do not explode. The duds are then later picked up by children or touched by a farmer's plow, and that contact then causes them to explode. See more at *www.uscbl .org/cluster-bombs*.

Call out litter bugs. Voice your exasperation when you see someone littering on our public paths, streets, or highways. Remind the individual that the planet belongs to all of us and we all share a responsibility to keep it clean. Also, littering is a misdemeanor offense in most communities that is punishable by a fine. It is a crime against the environment.

Become more accepting of your colleagues. People have different work habits, skills, and abilities. Resist the urge to criticize, demoralize, and demean. Instead, accept coworkers the way they are and for the talents and skills that they have.

Bring a game to your grandparent's retirement home. Meet regularly with your grandparent and others in his retirement home to play bridge, poker, mahjong, bingo, or some other board game. The point is to reach out to the one you love and bring people together.

Encourage a child to do his best. Provide him with the confidence to try to do new things, and help him if he needs it. Children who are encouraged to try their best and then succeed develop great self-confidence.

Host a party with a purpose. For a twist on the usual, make your next dinner or cocktail gathering a party with a purpose. Put out decorative boxes for donations, and theme the event around the charity that you're collecting for. For help choosing a worthy organization to donate to, visit *www .charitywatch.org* or *www.charitynavigator.org*.

Shop sweatshop-free. If you take a moment to research where your clothing comes from, you may be inspired to shop sweatshop-free. Organizations like No Sweat Apparel (*www.nosweatapparel.com*) are working to rid the world of sweatshops and promote a living wage for workers, one item of clothing at a time.

Help unload a neighbor's car. If you see a neighbor unloading his or her bags from the car after a shopping trip, offer to take them inside.

Boycott intolerant companies. Along with like-minded friends, refuse to support or give money to any organization, network, or company that practices bigotry, racism, or any other morally indefensible behavior.

Ready your house for a natural disaster. Anchor heavy furniture such as hutches, bookcases, and dressers to the wall to keep them from tipping over and potentially injuring someone if you live in an area of the country that experiences earthquakes.

Join the Peace Corps. This U.S. federal agency was established in 1960 according to the inspired vision of then Senator John F. Kennedy. He encouraged Americans to spread peace while working in underdeveloped countries. Today, the Peace Corps requires a commitment of twenty-seven months, and you must be at least eighteen years old. Visit *www.peacecorps.gov* for more information.

Keep in touch with family who live far away. Write to them often, call when you can, and send a long holiday card with photos. Tell them what you did this year, what life experiences you had, what new friends you made. Fill the card with words of good cheer and love.

Help bring education to those who need it. Make a donation to Asha for Education —and get your company to match your contribution. With your support, this organization helps to provide an education to underprivileged children in India. Visit its website (*www.ashanet.org*) for more information and to make your donation.

Join The Mobility Project. This organization helps serve those with disabilities in underprivileged countries. Visit *www.mobilityproject.org* for more information.

Prepare a hot drink for your mail carrier in winter. Ready a cup of cocoa, tea, or coffee, and have it waiting for the letter carrier out delivering mail on a cold and snowy day.

Write a letter. There are ways to help that take as little effort as picking up a pen. By writing a letter to your congress-person you can let him or her know that you are counting on them to help make a difference internationally. Many organizations even have sample letters you can use on their website. All you need to do is find the address of your local representative and mail it in.

Donate to the Campaign for a Nuclear Weapons Free World. This organization brings together advocates and organizations working on nuclear weapons issues to plan and collaborate on national campaigns. Check out its site at *www.nuclearweaponsfree.org* to learn more.

Send books to Africa. Through the organization Books For Africa (*www.booksforafrica.org*), you can donate books to be sent to countries in Africa.

Trick-or-treat for Unicef. Encourage the children in your life to trick-or-treat for Unicef each year. Not to worry: they can still get candy while trick-or-treating, but this way they're also helping to make a difference in the world. Unicef is a United Nations organization that helps children worldwide. Visit *www.forunicef.org/trickortreat/* for more information and to order the trick-or-treat for Unicef boxes.

Chaperone an outing at your teenager's school. Whether it's a ski trip or a weekend camping, be involved in your teen's life. Stay in the background with the other parents and don't embarrass her, but participate in the activities any way you can.

Become a volunteer teacher abroad. Similar to its medical counterpart, Teachers Without Borders sends volunteer teachers to countries that are lacking proper education. It also provides professional development for teachers worldwide. To sign up or sponsor a teacher, visit *www .teacherswithoutborders.org.*

Be mindful of the little things. Tell a neighbor, a visitor to the neighborhood, or a neighbor's family if you see a car parked with the lights left on, or a trunk or door open. Taking that extra minute to make sure they are aware could save your neighbor and their family a lot of time and money in the long run.

Volunteer with Habitat for Humanity. This and similar organizations build houses to shelter humankind. In order to rid the world of inadequate housing and homelessness, Habitat for Humanity seeks dedicated volunteers to assist in the effort. Find more information at *www.habitat.org*.

Save a quarter a day. While it might be hard to budget donating large lump sums to organizations, consider setting aside a quarter a day in a hunger fund. Once the quarters start to pile up, take them to the bank and then write out a check (see *www.bread.org* for donating to hunger organizations).

Clean a friend's garage. Take your broom, dustpan, and some garbage bags to a friend or neighbor's house and help them clean out their garage.

Become an animal advocate. Join the network of animal advocates working within the Humane Society of the United States, a grassroots organization seeking legal protections for animals against cruel treatment and suffering. See *www .humanesociety.org/about* for more information.

Be courteous in foreign airports and hotels. Have your phrase book handy and at least make an attempt to ask for what you need in the language of the country you are in. Most airport personnel are happy to help you, and you may discover that the individual helping you speaks English, but don't assume it.

Bring in a box of donuts for everyone in the office.

Encourage others to support local businesses. Spread the word to your neighbors about local businesses you have had good experiences with—help support them by word-of-mouth marketing.

Petition for a citywide recycling program. If your city or town does not have an established recycling program, make it happen. Get support from other eco-conscious citizens and petition your local politicians.

Set a good example for your children. Be respectful toward others and exhibit good manners. When you say "Yes, ma'am," and "Yes, sir," you are showing respect. Don't forget to say "please" and "thank you." In a bygone era, young people used to learn proper etiquette and manners in finishing schools. Now it is up to parents to teach youngsters how to conduct themselves in social situations.

Reach out to a child at risk. According to the United States Coalition for Child Survival, 30,000 children under the age of five die each day from treatable and preventable diseases, mainly diarrhea and pneumonia. The organization needs funding to continue its work on behalf of children. See *www .child-survival.org*.

Make a contribution to the World Health Organization (WHO). This is a branch of the United Nations that works to ensure good health for all humanity. Every minute, a mother dies in childbirth. The WHO has a program to safeguard mothers and newborns. Check out *www.who.int*.

Stop the proliferation of guns. If you are concerned about the role of weapons in domestic violence, school killings, and armed conflict in the world, join efforts toward tougher arms controls. Visit *www.controlarms.org* to see what you can do to stop gun violence.

Protest injustice wherever and whenever you see it. Get involved in stopping it. If you believe that all humans possess a disposition toward compassion and a sense of interconnectedness of us all, then fight for equal justice for everyone.

Volunteer your language services online. Do some good for the world using your writing or translating skills. Bilingual people are needed for translation work and other cyberspace tasks. Go to *www.onlinevolunteering.org* to sign up.

Send an impromptu thank-you e-mail. If a business associate goes out of her way for you, tell her how much you appreciate her unexpected kindness. While expressing your gratitude, mention how much your association with her means to you.

Cook for your dog. If you've ever read about tainted processed dog food, you might want to look into cooking natural dog food. This way you know exactly what your pooch is digesting each day.

Feed wildlife in winter. Leave out seeds, nuts, and other food that may appeal to the local wildlife during the colder months. This will help those not hibernating to survive in the dead of winter when the ground is frozen and seeds and berries are not as easily found.

Help vaccinate the poor. Join forces with Shared, a nonprofit, tax-exempt organization that works to increase the availability of vaccines and vital medicines to the world's poorest, whether in southern Africa, Armenia, or elsewhere. Shared aligns with other partners and individuals to accomplish its goals. For more information, go to *www.healthshares.org*.

Support international laws against child labor. Purchase carpets that have not been made using child labor. Certain countries like India and Nepal have in the past used child labor to do the fine-knot work of handmade carpets. To ensure your carpet has been made without child labor, look for the Rugmark label. Visit *www.skollfoundation.org* and *www.rugmark.org*.

Promote worldwide free speech. Support the work of international journalists who are monitoring the issues of press freedom, working to reduce censorship, trying to safeguard journalists (especially in war zones), publishing reports about press freedom, defending journalists, and protesting the imprisonment of journalists such as those considered cyber-dissidents by the Chinese government for writing on the Internet. For more information, see *www.rsf.org*.

Offer to help in your local library's children's section. Children who love stories are more likely to develop a love for books—and good reading skills help children perform better in school.

Make a donation in your friend's name.

Help rid the world of landmines. Raise money with your friends by hosting a dinner party and charging everyone an attendance fee. Donate the money you collect to ban landmines. Children are often the victims of landmine accidents. Roughly $100 can help a child with an amputated leg walk again. See *www.icbi.org* and click through to English-language site.

Stand in your spouse's shoes. Before you give in to the urge to let go a barrage of accusations and complaints against your life partner and lover, why not try to stand for a while in his or her shoes to get perspective. You might change your mind about launching the assault.

Stop the torture of POWs. Let your elected officials know that you are against your government conducting torture of POWs in violation of Article 5 of The Universal Declaration of Human Rights (1948), which states, "No one shall be subjected to torture or to cruel, inhuman or degrading treatment or punishment."

Become an employee of the United Nations. Be a professional policy advisor or worker in another specialized field of the UN. There are many different needs for more than 140 countries. There are a variety of jobs to be done requiring diverse skills. Such jobs include crisis prevention specialists to policy advisors, micro-credit specialists, and educators. See *www.jobsun.org*.

Support Food Not Bombs. Food Not Bombs is an organization that actively protests war and shares vegetarian food with the hungry at the same time. To donate food or money, or to learn more, visit *www.foodnotbombs.net*.

Help end global poverty. Make a donation to Make Poverty History. The organization offers a white wristband so you can raise awareness for the cause. Visit *www.makepoverty-history.org* to learn more about the organization and pledge your support.

Adopt a soldier. Make a commitment to send a care package to your soldier one to two times a month. To start an adoption, see *www.soldierangels.org*.

Prepare the next generation to keep the peace. Donate or volunteer with Seeds of Peace (*www.seedsofpeace.org*) and help develop the next generation of peacemakers.

Donate your old glasses. Gather up your old eyeglasses and donate them to Unite for Sight at *www.uniteforsight.org*. Americans toss out about approximately four million eyeglasses each year—eyewear that could benefit people in the developing world with vision loss.

Hug a girlfriend after her breakup. Honor her emotions, empathize with her pain, but resist telling her about your own breakups, offering platitudes, or giving advice. If she needs to talk, listen. If she needs to cry, give her tissues and hugs.

Help Iraqi women safely have their babies. The infant mortality rate and the maternal mortality rate (measured in deaths per 1,000) more than doubled in the years from 1999 to 2002. Access to proper nutrition, medical services, prenatal care, and vitamins ranges from restricted to nonexistent. Today, the United Nations Population Fund helps Iraqi women who are pregnant give birth in a clean place and, when needed, to get access to emergency obstetric care. For more information, see *www.unfpa.org/emergencies/iraq/index.htm*.

Lobby for living-wage jobs worldwide. Join efforts of others to call global governments into action and create jobs that pay a living wage jobs for everyone. Simply making sure everyone is fairly compensated for his or her work will cut down on worldwide poverty.

Link up with other like-minded people. Make an effort to meet other politically active people by attending political rallies, working with charitable fundraisers, and joining environmental groups for hikes, bird watching, or biking trips. When you join communities of like-minded people, you have more power to effect change, get laws enacted, and do good works.

Volunteer with Water for People. Dirty water is one of the leading causes of sickness in underdeveloped communities. Join the fight for clean water at *www.waterforpeople.org*.

Participate in a Relay for Life. Held by the American Cancer Society, these overnight events are held in cities and towns across the country. Check out the Relay for Life website at *www.relayforlife.org* and learn how you can form a team and participate in a relay in your area.

Help fight disease globally. Make a donation or volunteer with Doctors Without Borders (*www.doctorswithoutborders .org*). This organization provides much more than just vaccinations and medical care to communities that don't necessarily have the means to do so themselves. Visit their website for more information and to set up a monthly donation.

Advocate World AIDS Day. December 1 is World AIDS Day. Consider hosting an event in your community to raise awareness about the global impact of AIDS. At the event, hand out a list of organizations that help people suffering from AIDS worldwide so that people can choose to donate. Include organizations that specifically help women, help orphans displaced by AIDS, or help to find a cure. That way people can put their money where they feel the most passionately, instead of into an umbrella organization.

Be a pen pal to someone in service. No one wants to feel alone and forgotten. This is a way to help a soldier serving in a foreign land know he has a friend. Visit *www.emailour military.com* for more information on the program and learn how you can join.

Take a stand against genocide in the world. Educate yourself about how it happens and what can be done to stop it. Even after the horrors of the Nazi Holocaust, genocide has occurred in Darfur, Rwanda, Sudan, Iraq, and elsewhere. Check out *www.genocidewatch.org* to see how you can help.

Start your family's day with an inspiring quote. It will replay in their minds throughout the day and re-energize and motivate them toward their goals. Write it on a piece of paper and stick it on the fridge, tape it to the back door, or slip a copy into everyone's pocket—in short, make it accessible to read throughout the day so you can all become inspired.

Encourage countries to "Think Outside the Bomb." Several countries have already declared themselves nuclear weapons–free zones. Encourage other countries to do the same by visiting *www.peace-action.org*.

Help provide medical supplies to those in need. By volunteering with MedShare International (*www.medshare.org*) you can make sure that hospitals in developing areas of the world have the necessary medical equipment.

Volunteer to mentor young entrepreneurs. If you have business expertise that you could share with others, contact your local community small business organization to lend your support to entrepreneurs and owners of start-up companies.

Buy fresh eggs from a local farm. This will help both the farm and you. Your payment will be put to good use, helping with the daily maintenance and possible expansion of the farm. And the fresh eggs will taste better in your omelets, salads, and cakes.

Take off your shoes at the door. Wearing slippers or heavy socks indoors instead of shoes will prolong the time between the eco-damaging and expensive cleaning of carpets.

Decorate with reused items. Head to an architectural salvage yard before the hardware store to find fixtures, flooring, bars, banisters, and hardware supplies.

Adopt a teenager. There are many in the world who live in orphanages and foster care homes. Whether placed there as an abandoned or orphaned child, they started out in life already on an uncertain path. Usually, couples looking to adopt want a baby or young child, so orphaned teens are often the hardest to place.

Give away gardening supplies. Rather than throwing away the things you don't use anymore, choose to pass them on to other gardeners. Put potted plants, old firewood, unwanted gardening tools, bags of bulbs, and extra garden pots on the curb in front of your apartment or house with a sign that states: *Free for the Taking.*

Use environmentally friendly household cleaners. Many household cleaners on the market leave toxins in your environment (which in this case is your house!). Make the smart decision and use all-natural cleaning products such as Seventh Generation.

Become a part of your town's disaster relief team. When a natural disaster has hit or is about to hit your hometown, you can help out. Whether it's building sandbag walls or volunteering at evacuation centers, you can play an important role in everyone else's safety.

Give away your old dishware, pans, and utensils. Think of a single-parent family who may not have many household items or money to buy what they need. They'll appreciate your gift, and you'll have the satisfaction of knowing that your gift reduced the clutter in your kitchen.

Endow a scholarship at a local school. Start a scholarship program for local high school students looking to go college. As tuition prices keep increasing, everyone needs all the help they can get. You will need to contribute a significant amount of money for the principal endowment—the awards are then derived from interest on the principal sum—but it's worth it.

Teach an aged relative how to do seated stretching. These exercises will help him remain limber and keep his muscles toned. Put on some music that he likes and make it a pleasurable experience for you both.

Spend time with a child who has an absent family member. Your companionship will help fill empty hours and the void suffered by the child. Make it part of your commitment to that child and his family to be another stable and secure person in his young life.

Resist killing a helpful pest. Escort a honeybee, mosquito eater, or spider out the door rather than squashing them. The bee pollinates the garden, while the spider and mosquito eater consume pests and are therefore beneficial to your plants.

Buy milk in recyclable glass bottles. Instead of purchasing your milk in plastic or cardboard containers, opt for glass, which can be recycled or reused.

Hold a fundraiser to support a hospital. Organize family members of people who have received or are about to have an organ transplant. Together, plan a holiday boutique to sell all kinds of donated and hand-made items such as bird-houses, quilts, painted cookie tins, ornaments, and holiday napkin rings and table linens. Set up in the hospital lobby, and then donate the money to a particular hospital department that needs funds to buy specialized equipment or to enable a family without resources to stay near a loved one undergoing a transplant.

Volunteer at an animal rescue facility. You could do something as simple as answering the phones. Maybe dogs are your passion, and if so, consider joining other dog lovers to find homes for previously owned and rejected or abandoned animals. There are millions of dogs struggling to stay alive on the highways and byways of America.

Donate your old cell phones to charity. It's estimated that more than 150 million cell phones are lying around in office desk drawers and in homes. Check out *www.phones4charity.com*. Phones 4 Charity takes phones that work, as well as broken ones, recycling the latter in accordance with federal and local environmental standards.

Donate your old magazines to a school. Clean the clutter of magazines from around your house and donate those to a local school. Even if they are old, they can be used for art projects.

Try a different type of tree. Instead of supporting an industry that chops down pine or fir trees each year to use as Christmas trees, consider a potted herb, such as rosemary sheared in the shape of a holiday tree. Planted in a container, it will continue to grow.

Donate to the lupus research efforts. Join others in helping the Lupus Foundation of America conduct research to find a cure. Go to *www.lupus.org*.

Support an environmental cause. Figure out what you're really passionate about (water conservation, land preservation, recycling, etc.) and make a commitment of time, energy, and creative input. It might be elections of a local school board or a city issue of where to put a new parking lot that affects the local environment. Decide where you stand, and then get involved and do some good.

Opt for energy-efficient steel-belted radial tires. If inflated properly and regularly rotated, such tires can last over 100,000 miles. This will help cut down on rubber waste caused by disposal of old tires.

Give a child a summer job. The child could paint your fence, clear rocks from your garden, wash windows, or help you paint or repair an old bench. The point is to give a child something meaningful to do that enables her or him to earn a little money.

Read to the blind. You can help record audio versions of newspapers, books, and magazines for the visually impaired. Check out Learning Ally (*www.learningally.org*) today and volunteer.

Pick up trash. If you see litter, don't just let it bother you; get out there and pick it up! To read about one man's love of picking up trash, check out "Rob the Rubbish" and his story at *www.robtherubbish.com*.

Set up a fundraiser for school supplies. As schools struggle financially to pay for teachers, facilities, and supplies, parents are increasingly being asked to help out with classroom expenses. Education of our young is too important to ignore.

Participate in a disaster cleanup effort. Volunteer to help clean up debris after a tornado, earthquake, hurricane, flood, wildfire, or other natural disaster.

Give away your extra blankets. Look around your house for spare blankets and linens, and donate them to a community shelter for the homeless.

Volunteer at a suicide prevention phone bank. Help save the life of someone who is suffering and in deep distress.

Round up when you check out. Sometimes stores will have fundraising programs where you can round up your purchase price, donating the difference in change to a charity such as Autism Speaks. Even though it's less than a dollar, if everyone checking out at the store takes part, it can make a big difference to that organization.

Walk for breast cancer. Roughly 182,000 women receive a breast cancer diagnosis each year. A staggering 43,300 will die. Not only women, but also men, get breast cancer. Find a variety of ways to help fight this dreaded disease and visit multiple websites with information by logging on to *www .thebreastcancersite.greatergood.com*.

Keep your grocery shopping green. Buy fresh foods and eggs in cardboard containers—avoid Styrofoam. When Americans buy food, roughly one dollar of every eleven spent goes for packaging and much of it ends up in landfills.

Be frugal with water while brushing your teeth. Rinse to get the brush wet, and rinse to clean the brush when you have finished brushing. Don't leave the water running the whole time. Use only what you need. You'll soon discover that you don't really need much water to brush.

Help an at-risk teen go to college. Work with other professionals in your community to assist at-risk youth who may have the intelligence to do well in college but may not understand the application process or know how to find the resources to make it happen. You can make a difference in their lives.

Give up your window seat.

Write a thank-you note to a coworker. The next time he helps you with a project or a problem, take a minute to show your appreciation. A simple thank-you might do, but a note shows your appreciation at a whole new level.

Donate old books to schools. Look at your bookshelf and ask yourself if you're really ever going to reread each one. Schools can put used books to good use either through their loan system or by selling them at a used book sale and putting the profits toward buying new books.

Rally behind a local politician. Ask your friends and neighbors to join you in getting involved in local politics. Choose a candidate who will speak for you and your community, and help give a voice to those who have none and speak for those who can't.

Support the local police. Make a contribution to the police officers' association charitable foundation in your city. The money usually supports widow and orphan groups, college scholarships, youth leagues, drug resistance programs, victim support, and senior programs, among other worthwhile activities.

Close the worldwide health-care gap.
Support work being done by organizations
such as Global Health Council in its work
to narrow the gap between health care in
developing nations and that in richer ones.
Of special concern is the health of women
and girls, for whom the leading causes of
death are HIV/AIDS followed by malaria,
tuberculosis, and pregnancy and childbirth.
Visit *www.globalhealth.org* for more
information.

Give platelets. It takes a bit longer than donating blood (around one to two hours) but platelets are an important part of many life-saving surgeries.

Become a volunteer crossing guard. Some communities rely on volunteers to help kids get home safely. If your schedule allows, look into volunteering to fill this important position in the morning or afternoon.

Fight for art classes in schools. It is important for children to learn about the whole world and not just their little corner of it. With budget cuts and a focus on standardized testing, many school systems are cutting their art programs. Become an advocate for the children, and petition the school board if such a cut happens in your city.

Pass on your reading material. Take old magazines to a local hospital or a waiting room in a dentist's office.

Buy a cup of lemonade from a child's stand.

Give the gift of sight. Make a donation of any size to *www .sightsavers.org.* Your generosity could pay for a cataract operation to restore an adult's sight. A little bit more might buy a microscope for a hospital or train eye care workers. A sizeable donation could purchase an all-terrain vehicle for Sightsaver International's outreach program providing eye care for people who live in areas with rough terrain.

Establish a wildlife refuge in your garden. All you need to do is supply three things: a protected area where birds can nest, food (living plants as well as seeds, nuts, berries, suet, etc. that you supply), and clean water (bird bath, fountain, etc.). Watch as your little sanctuary fills with life and thrives.

Spoil your pet with an occasional treat.

Lobby a business to change its unfair policies. Start a letter-writing campaign or an e-mail petition. Think oil price gouging is going on? Believe our food is unsafe? Want medicines to be more affordable?

Align with others in a petition or e-mail campaign to bring your elected official's attention to the issue.

Give a gift from the March of Dimes. Visit the organization's website (*www.marchofdimes.com*) and browse its merchandise. Choose something that you know a loved one will enjoy and cherish. Purchase it and give it as a "just because" gift. You'll be brightening someone's day as well as improving the lives of thousands of babies.

Add baking soda to your washer load. This simple addition will reduce the amount of laundry detergent you will need to use by half. So you're releasing half as many chemicals into the environment every time you do a wash. It's a simple thing you can do to enhance the cleaning power of your wash.

Donate bookcases to a school library. If you have an old bookcase that's just collecting dust, contact your local school and see if they can put it to good use. Most schools are always looking for small pieces of furniture like bookcases.

Calm a fellow flier's nerves. Reassure someone on an airplane with you who fears flying. Offer to hold the hand of that person if he feels it would help. Do what you can to assuage his fear.

Give a good reference. If a coworker is seeking new employment, offer to write a letter of recommendation. Emphasize the good qualities and skills that individual possesses. Be truthful if the individual had shortcomings that affected his or her work, but don't be disparaging. Separate your emotion from the facts.

Take a child to the zoo. Talk with her about the rich diversity of animal life on our planet. Explain each animal's grooming habits, diet, method of bearing young, and natural habitat. Share insights into the role a particular animal plays in the ecological balance of the planet.

Rescue an injured bird. Sometimes birds fall from their nests or smash into glass windows. In both cases, retrieve the bird (avoid overhandling) and place it in a dry box until the bird recovers; then return it to the wild.

Donate a dog or cat bed to an animal shelter. These organizations often have small budgets. So little donations like a bed will go a long way to ensuring at least one animal's comfort.

Volunteer at a local hospital. Variously called Candy Stripers and Pink Ladies, volunteers (men are included, too) serve an important function in hospitals that are often understaffed. Volunteers can rock babies to sleep, operate the hospitality cart offering magazines and gum, fetch wheelchairs, and transport discharged patients to their cars.

Volunteer for the Gay and Lesbian Hotline.
Help callers who are struggling with fear,
depression, or are in some kind of distress
as a result of their sexual orientation. The
hotline number is 1-888-THE-GLNH; visit
www.glnh.org for more information.

Learn cardio-pulmonary resuscitation (CPR). Your knowledge and fast action could save someone's life. CPR is easy to learn. Courses are offered through local community colleges, park and recreation departments, and local branches of the Red Cross. You can even learn CPR from a video that has been approved for home training by the American Heart Association. Check out *www.cpr-training-classes.com* to sign up.

Establish an insectarium in your garden. Special seedlings that attract and support insects beneficial to your garden can be planted in a small corner of the space. For example, lupine and sunflowers attract small, beneficial wasps that prey on aphids, which are major pests in the garden. It's kind of like companion planting, but you are encouraging an "infestation" of the right kind of insects.

Mop with white vinegar and water. Next time you need to clean your linoleum floors, don't use expensive floor cleaning supplies. These may contain unduly harsh or toxic ingredients.

Learn to perform the Heimlich maneuver. Use it if you see someone choking, unable to cough up food or a foreign object. The simple procedure is easy to learn and could save a life. Teach it to your family and friends.

Turn your house green. Lend your support to the eco-friendly movement by making your house "green." Install solar panels for heat, and utilize rainwater collection and harvesting methods for water. When you renovate or repair your home, use recycled materials as much as possible. Get off the power grid and say goodbye to water bills.

Support mental health screening for teens. An organization called Teen Screen is run through Columbia University and makes free mental health checkups available to teens. Working with communities, the program enables teens to participate in screenings that are held in youth shelters, doctors' offices, schools, and youth groups in their cities and towns. For more information on how you can help its cause, visit *www.teenscreen.org*.

Fight malaria. This preventable and curable parasite-borne disease kills roughly a million people each year, ninety percent of them children in Africa. Malaria is caused by a parasite that is carried by mosquitoes and transmitted to people. Many of the world's poorest, especially woman and children, are at highest risk and, once infected, have little or no resources to deal with the disease. Find out more at *www .who.int/malaria*.

Join the effort to find a cure for an incurable disease. There are many from which to choose, including HIV/AIDS, many types of cancer, multiple sclerosis, autism, cystic fibrosis, polio, and Tay Sachs, to mention a few. Choose a disease, research how you can help, and get involved. Now make that cause your mission. Get off the couch, out of the house, and make your life count in the effort to save someone else's life.

Be an excellent witness. When you observe an accident or criminal activity, stay calm and out of danger. Memorize or take down vital information that would be useful for law enforcement. Share with the police what you have witnessed.

Join the Asthma Walk to help find a cure. More than 20 million Americans have asthma and nearly 4,000 die every year. Pollutants in the environment pose increased health hazards to asthma sufferers. Go to *www.lungusa.org* for more information.

Register to vote, and vote in every election. This is the right of every citizen over the age of eighteen. However, you should recognize it as a privilege and take advantage of the opportunity.

Work on behalf of immigrants and illegal aliens. Advocate for their humane treatment. Regardless of which side of the law they stand on, they are human beings and deserve the fair and just treatment that one member of humanity accords another.

Remind friends to get their checkups. Screenings can detect early breast cancer, colon cancer, prostrate problems, heart disease, and a number of other potentially life-threatening illnesses. However, many people put off getting health checkups and screenings. Don't let them.

Lobby for free rides for the homeless. Petition your community public transportation officials to provide free rides to the homeless who use public transportation.

Become involved with Al-Anon or Alateen. These are organizations that help those suffering from alcoholism. Help staff the Al-Anon hotline at 1-888-4-Al-Anon. A statistic provided on websites for recovering alcoholics states that each person's addiction to alcohol affects four other people. When a parent or teen is drinking, the entire family suffers. Find out more about how to be involved with Al-Anon or Alateen at *www.al-anon.alateen.org*.

Recycle e-waste. Many of the electronics you use in your daily life are harmful to the environment if they are just thrown away. Consider the impact of toxic e-waste in landfills and in the water supply. Make the choice to recycle these things instead. Visit *www.erecycle.org* to find an e-waste recycling facility close to you.

Volunteer at a local hospice organization. You will be supporting someone through the process of dying. Each person has to go through the stages of dying alone albeit often surrounded by family, friends, and a support team that will include a hospice nurse and doctor. A patient who is terminal has the right to use his own powers of reason and choice about his care and options as he lives each moment until death occurs. Find out more at *www.hospicenet.org*.

Help kids organize a fundraiser. One idea is to have a Christmas holiday boutique to raise money for a cause. They can paint wooden ornaments, glue on glitter, attach string, and sell their creations for a dollar each.

Return your neighbor's truck with a full tank. If your friend has been kind enough to allow you to use his vehicle, the least you can do is repay him by filling up the tank before returning his truck.

Let your boss know that you appreciate her. Perhaps she is particularly diligent, has great follow-through, comes up with terrific insights, or inspires creativity. Whatever her particular gift, let her know you admire her. It's probably surprising how infrequently she receives genuine admiration from her employees.

Fight juvenile diabetes. Donate to The American Diabetes Association and wear one of its red wristbands in support. For further information on the cause and to make a donation, visit *www.diabetes.org*.

Form a "mother of multiples" group. Offer support to others who are sharing similar experiences as parents of multiples. Together, you can save money by sharing baby clothes and other essentials, trade strategies about raising healthy children, and have play dates for the children when they become old enough for outings at the park and in other people's homes.

Turn off your air conditioner. Once a week during the summer, unplug all the air conditioners in your house. While this may make things warmer than usual, the benefits to the earth's atmosphere (and your electricity bill) are great. Spend the unplugged day outside in the shade.

Teach an arts and crafts class. Contact your local parks and recreation department. There is a need for interesting ongoing education that is fun for all ages. It's a good way to share your particular know-how with the school children of your town or city.

Support the work of Orbis in aiding the blind. Out of the 37 million people in the world who are blind, the humanitarian organization Orbis asserts that 28 million became blind unnecessarily because of lack of treatment and appropriate eye care. Orbis works to restore the vision of many in the developing world and to prevent blindness. See *www.orbis.org*.

Keep your neighborhood storm drains clear. Rake fallen leaves on the street in front of your home to keep them out of the storm drains. This will prevent flooding on your street during heavy rainstorms.

Be a volunteer for a mental health hotline. Give support and comfort to people in their time of great distress. Many times, these people just need someone to talk to. You can be that person.

Cut the plastic rings of any six-pack beverage carrier. Those plastic holders make it into the ocean where they are harmful to dolphins and other sea life.

Become a sponsor to a recovering addict. Whether they're in the process of conquering alcoholism or chemical addiction, these people still need help. There are support groups all over America and the disease is epidemic. These people need someone to walk the steps with them as they are recovering.

Make tiny hats for preemies. Donate these knitted caps to your local hospital or a family you know who's recently had a premature baby. Make the hats from washed and dried soft cotton. Call the hospital neonatal unit to find out if they have rules or criteria for making such items.

Get involved in community politics. Involvement is the only way to get your voice heard. Attend town meetings and help solve local homelessness, panhandling, and other problems that involve the entire community.

Support nonprofit organizations that aid senior citizens. Programs that believe in the importance of healthy, affordable, and ethical aging services for America's senior citizens are an important part of our society. One such organization offering a variety of services is the American Association of Homes and Services for the Aging. Visit *www.aahsa.org* for more information.

Make a donation to The Corps Network. This organization carries on the tradition of America's Civilian Conservation Corps in restoring the environment. For information on the organization and to learn how to donate, see *www.nascc.org*.

Eliminate standing water. Dump out stagnant water from birdbaths, tubs, pots, buckets, and cans on your property. Standing water provides a breeding ground for mosquitoes. Mosquitoes can carry dangerous diseases that can infect humans as well as their pets.

Recycle batteries instead of throwing them out. Batteries can be harmful to the environment if they are just thrown out with your garbage. Visit *www.batteryuniversity.com* to learn how to correctly dispose of them, and get your office, school, and church involved in their recycling.

Aid in hurricane disaster relief. Contribute to worldwide hurricane relief efforts through organizations such as Direct Relief. That organization has helped victims of disasters through partnerships with other organizations. It also provides assistance to health-care providers and financially strapped clinics. See *www.directrelief.org*.

Help your law enforcement officers unwind. Support crime-fighting organizations such as your local chapter of the National Police Athletic League. Check it out at *www .nationalpal.org* and make a donation.

Boycott unethical businesses. Refuse to conduct business with those that engage in immoral practices such as using offshore child labor, exploiting workers through low wages and putting them in harm's way, or forcing them to live in hazardous housing.

Host a family reunion. Gather everyone together and put out long sections of butcher paper and have everyone write out memories and family stories. Make it a day focused around genealogy, family togetherness, and the making of a new tradition, the reunion of the family held at regular intervals throughout your life.

Throw a fundraiser and donate the proceeds. Convince a local business to join with you in planning, sponsoring, and hosting a high tea, a black-and-white ball, a summer wine tasting and dinner, or a music concert. Donate the money raised to a charity.

Recycle your old motor oil. Annually, millions of gallons of used oil pollute America's waterways. Even if you throw the oil into the garbage (which is prohibited by many cities and towns), the stuff ends up in landfills and eventually gets back into the groundwater. Visit *www.recycleoil.org* to learn how.

Help provide safe drinking water for children. According to the World Health Organization, more than 3.4 million lives, mostly young children, are lost each year because of water-related diseases, the leading cause of death worldwide. Four thousand children die each day because of diseases related to the organisms thriving in the filthy drinking water they consume. Find and fund programs for safe drinking water.

Host a charity fundraiser for a health-related cause. Whether it's an informal potluck hosted at your house, or a black tie event at a fancy restaurant, you can bring your friends, family members, coworkers, and neighbors together for a good cause. Collect donations at the door or charge per plate, and then donate all the proceeds to a world health cause.

Purchase some gifts for displaced children.
Children—whether toddlers, preadoles-
cents, or teenagers—suffer in unimaginable
ways when removed from their families and
placed in shelters. Visit your local children's
shelter. Find out its needs. Help the children
placed there in whatever ways you can.

Donate to charitable consignment shops. De-clutter your house and give unwanted items to a local thrift store that is associated with a local mental health center if there is one. Some communities have thrift stores to benefit the Cancer Society or Catholic charities or mental health centers for kids.

Notify neighbors about severe weather warnings.

Support the National Runaway Switchboard. Its mission is to keep kids safe who have run away from home, are thinking about it, or are at-risk. The goal is to keep kids off the streets. The program also will help a runaway return home through its Home Free program. See how you can help at *www.1800runaway.org*.

Collect spare change for disaster victims. You'd be surprised how much change many people have lying around the house. If everyone pooled together the loose change (or change cups) that they find, a huge difference could be made for disaster relief. For help getting organized collecting change, visit *www.changeforchange.org*.

Become a volunteer firefighter. Help support the first line of defense that protects your community in the case of a fire. Pledge your time, hard work, and willpower to your local volunteer firefighting force. Check out *www.nvfc.org* for more information on the volunteer force.

Aid flood-prevention crews. Join the sand-bagging team, filling and distributing sandbags before the local river crests and floods outlying areas. Help homeowners and friends who own businesses in your community board up windows and doors.

Help a wounded animal. Stop and call for aid if you see an animal wounded in a vehicle accident. Contact a local wildlife shelter or emergency veterinarian clinic.

Open your home to those displaced by disaster.

Get involved in your community's Citizens Corps Council. The work of the council is to keep communities safe from disasters, terrorism, and crime. The organization, a component of the U.S. Freedom Corps and coordinated by the Department of Homeland Security, encourages local citizens to participate in setting up programs, developing plans of action, locating local resources, and assessing threats to their communities. For more information, visit *www.ready.gov/ citizen-corps*.

Give away what's in your closets. Donate unwanted coats, shoes, sweaters, jeans, and other items that you no longer use to a local shelter or charity.

Help at a local soup kitchen. Don't wait until Thanksgiving or Christmas (when many people volunteer at soup kitchens). Find one in your community that needs volunteers, and start this week.

Rescue disaster-displaced pets. During natural disasters, many animals become lost. Keep them safe until help arrives or until they can be transported to an animal shelter.

Take a self-defense class with a family member. Learn how to protect yourself or defend someone else.

Support your local battered women's shelter. Donate time, money, or household goods. Domestic violence is epidemic in America. If the cause is one that speaks to your passion, help any way you can to stop the violence. Call a women's shelter and find out what it specifically needs. Get friends and family to help you provide what is needed.

Prepare for a disaster. Check out the Department of Homeland Security's disaster preparedness website. There you can find ideas to prepare your kids and your business for unexpected disaster. See *www.ready.gov*.

Give coats and jackets to relief organizations. Go through your closets and find the ones you no longer wear. Put them in a box and donate them in order to help people in cold climates—even the homeless in North American cities and towns—survive the cold weather.

139

Organize a neighborhood food drive. Get your neighbors to donate canned and nonperishable goods, and give everything collected to a local food bank. Why not make this an event that is not tied to a holiday? Hungry people need food at all times of the year.

Help out children who live on the streets. Whether you donate or volunteer, you can give these street youths some choices, skills, and opportunities for a better life and healthier future. Check out *www.streetkids.org*.

Sign up with *www.upromise.com*. As a member of UPromise®, a percentage of a number of your daily purchases will go to building a college fund for a student of your choice. Set up your account, start spending, and start funding a brighter future for a child in your life.

Volunteer to work at the Special Olympics. There are many tasks for volunteers, including serving as drivers, athlete escorts, presenters, scorekeepers and timers, fundraisers, coaches, officials, first aid personnel, and more. Click on the "volunteer" icon at *www.specialolympics.org*.

Volunteer with Meals on Wheels. This national organization brings meals to elderly people so they do not go hungry. See what you can do to help out the cause by visiting its website at *www.mowaa.org*.

Wave hello to your neighbors.

Bring your neighborhood together. Rally around a common cause such as beautifying your street or working on a community garden project in your apartment house complex. Establish a planning committee to arrange for a garden party. Invite everyone in your neighborhood to view the flowers. Serve lemonade and homemade treats. It's a good thing to do for building community. When neighbors know neighbors, they can watch out for each other and their property.

Support your local film festival. Many cities and even small towns now have film festivals. Become part of the experience by volunteering time or expertise. Many actors in Hollywood were once kids who loved watching films. Be a force for bringing film into your community.

Donate public transit tickets to local charity groups. Save your tickets with unused minutes remaining on them, and give them to these charitable organizations. They collect the tickets and return them to the transit company for higher-priced tickets. Those are then disseminated to low-income or homeless workers.

Help an older relative register their prescriptions online. These services are often less expensive, and they offer door-to-door service, so your loved one does not need to leave his or her house. However, make sure he or she knows the facts about buying prescription medicines over the Internet. Visit the U.S. government's fact sheet with him or her at *www.publications.usa.gov*.

Give your mother a "gifts of the self" coupon book. Include coupons for a dinner you will make for her, a facial that you will personally give her, a foot and leg massage with some scented oil, and other ways to spend time showering love upon her. Staple your coupons together and present them inside a card. It's perfect for Mother's Day and birthday gifts.

Volunteer to be the Santa at a children's shelter. Dress up as Old Saint Nick and take some time to bring holiday cheer to those who need the most cheering up. Organize a toy drive among your family, friends, and coworkers, and bring a sack of presents with you.

Offer city workers some water. Next time you have work being done in your neighborhood by city workers, offer them all nice cold glasses of water. It's a great way to boost their spirits and productivity.

Help an elderly neighbor clean her yard. Rake up any leaves, trim her hedges, and mow her lawn. Remove fallen dead tree limbs and brush from her yard. Tree limbs and brush can become a fire danger.

Volunteer to be a translator. Whether it is at a school, church, the office, or even at the grocery store, your ability to translate and communicate in another language will prove useful. Just see the need and fill it.

Welcome new neighbors. Start a committee to greet new families moving into your neighborhood. Make sure everyone takes some time to go over to the new neighbors' house to introduce themselves. A strong reception to newcomers says, "Come into our community and be part of our family."

Buy a homeless person a hot meal. It doesn't have to be an expensive sit-down dinner. A hungry person needs nutrition and nourishment of the body and soul. The face of homelessness in America includes families with children. Poverty is frightening for many of us because deep down we may fear a reversal of fortune in our own lives.

Recommend someone for a local board. Write a letter of introduction for someone you know who seeks to serve on a local community board or charitable foundation. If someone desires to serve and needs such a letter, and you are in a position to write it, then do it because both the board and the person who wants to serve on it benefit.

Help your family live more simply. We collect too much clutter in our lives, buy things we seldom truly need, and suffer from *consumer-itis* with its inevitable side effect of credit card debt. Buying things offers a short-lived joy; it does not bring lasting happiness. Eliminating unnecessary monthly expenditures will help you and your family.

Help someone cross a busy street. Be it a woman navigating a stroller with other children in tow, an elderly person with a bag of groceries, a man with a white cane, a child on a bike, a homeless veteran with a shopping cart, or anyone else who looks like he or she could use a little help—offer them some help.

Organize a neighborhood open forum. Start an informal discussion group to air neighborhood issues of concern. Focus on constructive problem solving. Without alienating anyone or discounting any neighbor's ideas, engage in vigorous debate and explore all possible solutions.

Help with the after-storm response. Report downed power poles, trees, and electrical lines that are casualties of a storm. They pose a dangerous public-safety hazard. If you have elderly neighbors, help to clear their yards of fallen branches and other debris once the storm is over.

Buy groceries for a mom on welfare. Our rich country is full of poor, single moms struggling to put food on the table for their children. If you see a woman with her child counting out food stamps in a grocery store line coming up short, pay the difference if you have the means. Suggest to her that someday when her situation is improved, she can do likewise for someone else.

Install a window box for a bedridden neighbor. Being able to see flowers blooming beyond a window can bring joy and affirm the natural cycle of life. This simple act will help bring the outside in for someone who can't enjoy the beauty of the outdoors.

Be a better parent. If you are expecting or already have a child, why not take a parenting class to learn about the kind of behavior to expect from children in various age groups. You will learn about discipline, time-outs, rewards, childhood self-esteem, and how to emphasize behaviors you want repeated while de-emphasizing others.

Help put an end to childhood poverty in America. Children are starving right here in our country, in your state, and possibly even in your city. Don't brush this off as just a third-world issue. Make a donation to the National Center for Children in Poverty to help these kids receive the financial support they need. Visit the center's website at *www .nccp.org*.

Participate in career day at your local high school. Volunteer to talk about your career and inspire young teens to enter your field of work.

Support the work of The Hesperian Foundation. The non-profit publisher produces books about health for people with little formal education. The books, simply written and illustrated in a collaborative process involving people from around the world, are made available for distribution within communities where there might not be a doctor or health-care professional. See *www.hesperian.org*.

Attend a local school's fundraiser. These events raise money for a particular student group. Whether the school is sponsoring a performance of a well-known play to raise money for the theatrical department or hosting a spaghetti dinner to raise money for the band, enjoy an evening at your local school and help the students reach their financial goals.

Support domestic violence centers. These organizations work on behalf of victims of domestic violence such as the National Center for Children and Families (NCCF). The center not only helps homeless families, it also provides services to neglected and abused children and teens, as well as victims of domestic violence. For more information, visit *www.nccf-cares.org/donate.htm*.

Let the neighborhood kids play in your yard.

Plan a big family vacation. Invite the family members who have grown up, moved away, and had children of their own. Invite aunts, uncles, cousins, grandparents, and great-grandparents. Choose a destination like Hawaii or Disneyland. Make it a family reunion in a place where everyone can find something to do.

Join the graffiti-fighting team in your city. Neighborhood walls, dumpsters, and businesses look dreadful after being tagged by miscreants. Do your part to help beautify your community.

Mow your neighbor's yard. If you have promised in the past to mow another person's yard and forgot, write yourself a note and make a point to follow through upon your promise. Do the honorable thing. How much extra effort is it really?

Invite a lonely neighbor over for coffee. Include that individual in activities involving your friends and family. Sometimes people choose isolation instead of seeking companionship because they feel they are intruding in others' lives.

Make a wish come true for a sick child.
Youngsters with life-threatening illnesses
are the most in need of special attention.
See Wish.org to see how you can help a
child's dreams become reality.

Volunteer to teach a vocational class at a local shelter. While donations of food and clothing are always helpful, those of the "teach a man to fish" philosophy might consider donating their time and skill by teaching a vocational class at a local shelter. This could be anything from job interviewing skills to typing to carpentry.

Wash a neighbor's car. If you already have everything together to clean your car, why not offer to wash your neighbor's as well? Have them pull into your driveway or onto your lawn, and scrub away. If you have him park on the lawn, you'll be giving your yard a deep soak at the same time.

Sort food at a local pantry. After all of the donations come spilling in, there needs to be someone there to sort out what's good and what's bad. Believe it or not, some people try to donate already-opened food items. A couple of hours can go a long way in a food-sorting facility, making sure that those in need are getting the best of the donations.

Expand your friends' vocabularies. Teach all your friends a new word every day or week. Leave a daily vocabulary message on your refrigerator, or send out an e-mail to your friends and family. Use the new word in your communications with them. This is something that will help them in their personal and professional lives.

DARE to keep kids off drugs. The DARE program goes into schools and teaches kids not to do drugs. Help out with this worthy cause by donating time or money.

Save your dollars and put them to work for you. Meet with a financial planner at the bank, get advice from an expert or a certified public accountant, or make your hobby learning about how to build wealth.

Donate unused makeup to a woman's shelter. Women in this type of situation need all the cheering up they can get. Help them feel pretty by donating your unused makeup. It will help lift a woman's spirits to have a little box of lipsticks, cheek blush, and powder to experiment with on her own skin.

Crochet items for a senior care center. Create some lap blankets for elderly people and donate them to a local nursing home. Your gifts will help warm their legs and their hearts.

Volunteer at a senior citizen center. Visit a senior citizen housing complex and offer to teach a workshop on a subject you know well. Such complexes often have a library or a music room or a place where seniors can gather for such a presentation. You will be sharing your knowledge with people who may not get out to lectures like they used to, and you may well have a captive audience of people intensely interested in your subject.

Let a sibling borrow something special. Lend your sister your favorite lipstick. Or make her day and let her borrow whatever she wants from your makeup drawer or closet.

Offer to pick up food for a neighbor. On your next trip to the grocery store, see if anyone needs anything before you go. It saves time for the neighbor and keeps one more car off the road.

Mentor a local women's group. Share your skills with a woman or group of women. If you feel you don't have the skills, help them find other women who are experts in what they are trying to do or accomplish. Find other women willing to be mentors.

Help control neighborhood pests. Keep the local pest and wildlife population at bay by vigilantly picking up fruit that has fallen from trees and berries plucked from plants or vines. Roof rats and raccoons love those kinds of foods.

Be prompt about paying your bills. Maintain a good credit score and nearly every business will want your patronage. Take responsibility for your debt when you incur it.

Make sure relatives' medications are taken as prescribed. Accidental overdoses of prescription drugs resulting in death are on the rise. Be cognizant of what medications your parents and grandparents are taking and how often. Ask your doctor about consequences of adding any new prescription into their regimen before they start taking any new pills.

Tithe ten percent of your income. Donate it to your church or favorite local charity. If you have the money and can spare some to put to work for others who have none, then consider making a tithing commitment. If your income increases, think about giving more.

Put your extra change in an expired parking meter. As you're walking through your city center, check and see if anyone is parked at an expired meter. Pop a few coins in. If you have ever received a parking ticket, you probably have wished that someone had done that for you.

Repair an elderly neighbor's house. Find a way to put carpenters and others together with organizations that can help with funding. Repair the house or raise up a new one so that the elderly occupant is safe again.

Compliment a family member who has accomplished something. Your recognition will likely mean more than any ribbon, badge, certificate, or trophy that he will receive.

Purchase a special license plate for your car. Many states have a program where you can show your support for different causes on your license plate, with a portion of the cost of the plate donated to a charity. Next time you get new plates consider this option; causes taking part in this vary by state but often include breast cancer and the environment.

Help a legal immigrant become a citizen. Make sure she understands all the requirements for citizenship, and help her study for her citizenship test. Drive her to take the immigration test or to be sworn in as a U.S. citizen.

Housesit for a friend while she goes on vacation. She will have peace of mind about her home (and possibly pets, if you are watching them as well) and can focus on her much-needed vacation.

Water your vacationing neighbor's lawn. During a hot spell, turn on his sprinkler or bring yours over to his lawn. A thoughtful act like this will save your neighbor the effort and money it takes to replant a burnt lawn.

Offer to pick up the mail and newspapers. When your neighbors go on a weekend trip, see if they want you to collect these delivered items. Newspapers piled up in a driveway and mail stuffed into an overfull box signals that no one is home. The house could become a target for burglars.

See opportunity everywhere. We live in an abundant universe. Opportunity isn't something that comes once in a lifetime; it may appear several times a day. Expect it, see it, and seize upon it. It's meant for you. Other people will have their own opportunities.

Support your local high school's car wash. Get your car washed by high school students during their car wash fundraiser. While it might not get your car as clean as a professional wash, your contribution will make a difference and help the community's schools.

Set up a companywide recycling program. If your company doesn't have a recycling program in place, work with your Operations Department to make it happen. Help to get quotes from local recycling plants and see which one would offer your company the best deal.

Take a volunteer vacation. Spend your time off helping others. Team up with an organization like the Sierra Club (*www .sierraclub.org*) and go out on a service trip. The reward of seeing the faces of those people whose lives you've brightened will be compensation enough.

Help novice travelers. If you are a seasoned traveler, help someone who is new at it and who may be a little apprehensive. Offer calm reassurance. Help them understand the process of checking in, changing planes, disembarking, going through customs, etc.

Help search for a lost child. Nothing could be more frightening than not knowing where your child has gone. Whether the child has just fallen asleep in the backyard where no one can see him, or has run away and has become the focus of a police investigation, the child must be found and the family supported in their distress.

Adopt a pet from an animal rescue organization. Check out organizations such as Tony LaRussa's Animal Rescue Foundation (ARF) at *www.arf.net*, *www.secondchancedogs.org*, or *www.petfinder.com*. Do your part and give a loving home to a helpless animal.

Support companies that give to charities. Peruse programs, catalogs, and brochures at your favorite cultural, charity, or sporting event for names of sponsors and products to purchase. Choose to patronize those that donate to your favorite charities.

Give excellent directions to someone who is lost. Keep it simple and clear, and don't talk too fast. For someone just passing through or visiting your community for the first time, getting lost is not fun. Put a friendly face on your entire community by making the visitor feel welcome in your town. Give directions and perhaps the name of a great restaurant nearby or the closest gas station.

Stay at an environmentally conscious hotel or inn. These are places that are taking that extra step to protect the environment while serving you. For a full list visit *www.greenhotels.com* or, if you've already made a reservation, call ahead and ask.

Offer to baby-sit your neighbor's kids for free.

Help a neighbor paint his house. It's a big job and if the home-owner is trying to do it alone, offer a helping hand. The work will proceed much faster with four hands than with two.

Read to kids at a shelter. If you're looking for a regular volunteering gig but can't find one that suits your needs or schedule, create your own. Call your local homeless or women's shelter and ask if you could come in for one hour each week to read to any children who might be staying there.

Get your company to donate its frequent flier miles. How many conferences and business trips does your company send you and your coworkers on? See if your bosses would be interested in donating the frequent flier miles that have been accumulated. Several of the airlines will take your miles to help children in need and their families. See sites like *www.wish.org* for more information.

Get an animal I.D. band or collar for your pet. Consider also having a veterinarian insert an I.D. chip. These measures often prove helpful in recovering a lost pet and help animal rescue services identify animals they find on the streets.

Live by the Golden Rule. Treat others with the same love you would give yourself and members of your family. It's a simple idea, but one that will have a positive effect on everyone you come in contact with.

Walk your dog regularly. It's an easy task, but one that is often overlooked or ignored. Make it a routine daily outing. Your dog will look forward to it and it is healthy for you both.

Say thank you to your bus driver.

Make a wedding album for a recently married friend. Use the pictures you took with your own camera, the wedding invitation, images of their cake, a CD with the song played for their first dance, and one of the favors with their initials on it, and put them all together in an album for their first anniversary. Buy scrapbook cutouts, stickers, and fancy papers to add special touches or enhance the wedding/marriage theme.

Talk to your company about matching funds. Some companies have a policy of matching employee donations to various charities. If your company doesn't have this program, talk to your supervisor about implementing one.

Be a good traveling companion. Some small European hotels offer private rooms but shared bathrooms. Don't park yourself for hours doing makeup in a bathroom that must be available to several other travelers.

Visit a shut-in with your cat or dog. Animals seem to have a therapeutic healing affect on people who are ill, lonely, disabled, or forgotten. Take your well-behaved pet with you when you visit a friend or relative who stays away from people. Watch how she interacts with your pet and how it cheers her up.

Carpool. Share your ride to and from work with coworkers. Cutting down on auto emissions and reducing the use of fossil fuels are good things we can do for the planet.

Telecommute. Ask your boss if telecommuting might be an option for you on one or more days each week. This will get your car off the road, which helps the environment.

*Buy cough drops for
a sick coworker.*

Be a crisis coach. If a friend is going through an extremely rough time, call him every evening at a set time to check on how he's doing and to find out if he needs anything or just wants to talk.

Practice good cell phone etiquette. Do you *really* want everyone in the office to hear every word you tell your friend about your ugly encounter with your ex, the wild weekend with the in-laws, or the night of great sex with your new man? Put your phone on the vibrate setting and make a note of who is calling. Return the call later in a more private environment.

Take care of yourself if you are pregnant. The most important person to do well by is your child. Get prenatal care, take vitamins, eat well, abstain from alcohol, stop smoking, do stretches (such as yoga), exercise (walking and swimming are good), eat well, and do everything in your power to ensure the life you are carrying will come out healthy and strong.

Understand that life is all about choices and consequences. You will live a better life once you realize every action you take causes a reaction. At times, you may feel that you have no choice, but the truth is that you do. In fact, not making a choice is still a choice. Stand on moral high ground and make good choices whenever possible.

Volunteer at a local animal therapy group. Some places employ animals (for example, horses) in therapy with people in need of healing. Set aside some time to help these organizations out by providing some of your time free of charge.

Help a grieving friend. Listen to your heart for inspiration and do what you can to lighten that friend's burden. When someone loses a spouse or family member, he or she may shut out others, stop eating, and retreat from the world. Help the grief-stricken person during one of his or her most challenging life transitions. See how it changes your perception of what's important in life.

Be conscious of your behavior when abroad. Have you ever looked around when in a foreign country and been able to pick out who is American and who isn't? Be aware of how local people are acting in certain situations, such as sitting in a coffee shop, and make an effort not to stand out as an outsider.

Listen and learn from your opponents. Be open to the ideas of your adversaries and opposites. They might stimulate ideas in you that you might never have had without the give and take of creative conversation and brainstorming.

Take care of a distressed friend's pet. Offer to brush, feed, walk, or bathe a friend's pet when your friend is in a crisis. An emotional crisis can drain away energy, leaving the owner too exhausted to properly care for the animal.

Make your office an Earth Share work-place. Start a campaign in your company to get the business involved with Earth Share. Participants pledge a certain amount of each of their paychecks to the cause. Visit *www.earthshare.org* for more information.

Keep work at work. Endeavor to keep your career from taking over all the available time in your life. Every life needs downtime. Without rest and relaxation, your life is out of balance. Career concerns are always important; however, keep them in balance with the other needs in your life.

Clean up after your animal. Pick up your dog's poop when you are out walking with him or her. It's mandatory in some communities. Tuck a plastic bag or paper sack into a pocket on your way out for the walk, and use it when your dog does his business.

Build or buy a birdfeeder. After filling it, remember to regularly clean it to avoid the spread of avian infections. If you fill your feeder with bird food that attracts songbirds, you'll enjoy listening to the songs of your newly found feathered friends and watching them flock to your feeder at feeding times.

Protect your loved one's lungs from toxic fumes. When you are painting or staining wood furniture, make sure there is adequate ventilation. If possible, do the work in a garage with the door open. This way you and your family members or roommates aren't breathing in the harmful fumes.

Say "no thanks" to fresh linens daily. Some hotels have a system where only towels left on the floor will be replaced with new ones. Think about how often you wash your towels at home and decide if you really need fresh ones daily; you'll be doing the environment a favor by reusing.

Save electricity and dine al fresco. On a warm summer evening, set up a table in the garden, courtyard, or backyard. Burn citronella to keep the mosquitoes away. Make the table pretty, dressing it up with special linen, china, and flatware. Prepare a special meal with the freshest summer ingredients and serve it with a fine bottle of wine.

Be a support person for a caregiver. A caregiver's life is filled with hard labor and emotional ups and downs that can take a devastating toll on her health. Being a friend and support person for a caregiver is one of the most important roles you can fulfill.

Brighten up your workplace. Make suggestions to your boss about improving the lighting in your work area. About sixty-eight percent of workers complain about the light in the workspace, according to a study done by interior designers working with Cornell University. Read more about workplace lighting in the "See the Difference" article on *www.oneworkplace.com*.

Give money to a friend. Drop an extra twenty-dollar bill into an envelope and send it anonymously to a friend of a friend who is a single mom or dad and struggling to make ends meet.

Practice yoga with someone you care about. Yoga should not be militaristic. Stretches should be gentle and prolonged as tolerated. The emphasis is on relaxing into peace, attuning to the body's wisdom and guidance, and establishing the time and means for relaxation, strengthening, and healing to occur.

Refrain from confronting intolerable travelers. If you find that during a flight a nearby seatmate has drunk too much alcohol, is using offensive language, and is becoming obnoxious, let a flight attendant know. You will be speaking up for everyone in your section. Ask her to find you another seat. If there are no others, spend some time out of your seat walking or standing in the galley if it is safe to do so.

Take time to meditate each day. You may only have five minutes to spare in your busy schedule but take it for yourself. Turn within. Tune out the world and your five senses. Sink deep into the quiet and deepest place of Self and feel the inner peace.

Return phone calls and e-mails promptly. It shows respect for the caller and writer. Otherwise you are making that other person sit around and wait to hear from you.

Make holiday cards green. Encourage your office to send a holiday e-card this year rather than wasting paper by mailing out paper greeting cards.

Eat less meat. On average, it costs much more to raise a herd of animals (feed, supplements, land, shelter, veterinarian costs, etc.) than to raise a field of beans or corn or to produce other nonanimal sources of protein. The Federal Food and Drug Administration states that to eat for a healthy heart, you must cut down consumption of trans fats and saturated fats, most often found in food from animals. Eating less meat is a good thing to do for your body and the planet.

Remain calm. Practice patience and serenity by counting to ten or following the breath in and out. Such practices help to provide a counter-balance to the effects of daily stress.

Protect your child against skin cancer. Caused by the sun's harmful ultraviolet rays, it can be prevented by making sure he wears a wide-brimmed hat and is covered with a good sunscreen with an SPF rating of at least 15 over exposed parts of his body before going outdoors.

Be mindful of competitors. Strive to be the best but don't bring down someone else to get to the top. Personal gain is nothing if accomplished at a cost to others.

Notice the good and offer praise. If you notice a coworker is remarkable in some way, take the time to tell them. It takes only a few seconds to say a couple words of praise, but it will make that person's day and help them to be more productive.

Keep the noise level down. When staying in small family-owned hotels or apartments in Europe and Asia, turn radios and televisions down when people would ordinarily be going to bed or are already sleeping. Be respectful of others sharing the facility. Don't let children run wild and jump on beds. Avoid talking loudly or yelling.

Set out a bowl of candy for everyone in the office to share.

Give a loved one a foot massage. Nothing feels better at the end of a long day or grueling workweek. Don't do it because you expect one in return; do it because you want to help your loved one relax.

Support local chapters of women's business organizations. These organizations help career-minded women and women-owned businesses thrive and prosper. Most groups offer lectures, networking, and informational events and promote economic alliances. They trade information, build strategic alliances, and effect policy changes that affect women-owned businesses. Find out more at the Small Business Administration's Office of Women's Business Ownership at *www.sba.gov*.

Create a healthier work environment. Ask your manager or boss to monitor the air quality where you and your coworkers spend the greatest part of your workday. Chemical contaminants in the environment can make people sick. Worse, they can lead to permanent health issues, causing lower productivity and higher medical expenses.

Help a coworker think creatively. Sometimes it's easier to think outside the box with another person. The next time he meets a roadblock in his career path, sit with him and discuss possible solutions to his problem. Two heads coming up with a variety of ideas on how to navigate such impediments can be better than one.

Stop being habitually critical and negative. It spreads like a disease, infecting everyone in your office with whom you have contact. Don't just break the bad habit; replace it with a good habit that includes lots of positive thinking and words of support for those with whom you work.

Report suspicious behavior. Pay attention to who is around you, whether you are on a plane, in an airport, on a subway, or at a crowded event. A heightened awareness is a good thing to have in today's world.

Help a coworker unload boxes of office supplies. Carrying in boxes of paper, toner cartridges, pens and pencils, paper clips, and the stuff that keeps offices running can be drudgery, but a helping hand makes it go faster.

Be courteous to those serving you. Remember to tip the domestics, waiters, captain, sommelier, rest room attendant, doorman, and limousine driver. When you are planning a vacation and the budget for it, don't forget to factor in some tipping.

Refill the copier's paper tray. The next time you use your office copier, put more paper in the paper tray. This simple act will save someone else time when they go to make copies and don't have to worry about being out of paper.

Learn how to give positive criticism and feedback. Giving and receiving criticism is not easy. Finding fault is easy, but finding fault isn't the point. Offer honest criticism in private. Be calm and thoughtful when making your point. Show a spirit of concern and a desire to help. If it's a project that is the focus of the criticism, explain what isn't working and why. Focus on the problem, not the person. Offer suggestions for fixing the problem or making the project better. Solicit feedback to make sure the other person understands the point you are making.

Buy from local businesses when you travel. Doing so means you are supporting a local economy. Buy original art from artisans painting in a lane in France, bread from a boy with loaves on his bike in a Russian village, or thangka or scroll-paintings from monks in Nepal.

Invest in socially responsible mutual funds.
It's a way to do some social good while
putting your money to work for you. Ask
your investment banker or counselor to suggest socially responsible funds that are con-
sistent with your level of risk.

Be a foster caregiver to an abandoned animal. If you cannot adopt but could provide interim shelter, food, and veterinarian care for a helpless animal, consider being a foster care provider.

Surprise your lover with breakfast in bed.

Limit the time you spend on the Internet. The Internet has expanded all kinds of possibilities in life for all of us. But be aware of how much time on the Internet is productive and how much is wasteful. Don't let the Internet become a substitute for real-world relationships.

Establish five charitable goals for your company. Set a list of priorities for giving this year and get your company involved in helping achieve these generous acts. Spread your generosity out among different groups and organizations.

Step aside for those with connecting flights. Let someone cut in front of you if they have to make a connecting flight and you don't. Sometimes, to get from one flight to another or to change airlines, you have to get off the plane and literally run to another gate. Missing a connection is a major headache.

Put up fliers for a lost pet. The time you spend helping to find the lost animal will benefit both pet and owner. Make a difference by donating your time and commitment to helping to bring that animal home.

Be a safe driver. Resist the urge to express road rage when a tense driving situation calls forth such urges. Instead of giving inconsiderate drivers the finger, slamming on your horn, yelling at your kids, or chewing out an employee when you get to work or the person who nabs the parking spot in front of you, count to ten and breathe deeply. Redirect the urge to lash out by counting and breathing deeply.

Brush your pet's teeth. Oral health is as important for your animals as it is for you. Insist on dental health checkups along with their regular veterinarian visit.

Buy shatter-resistant sunglasses for your children. Children spend more time outside in the sun than adults do, so parents need to pay attention to their children's vision and must schedule regular eye exams. You need to protect their eyes against harmful ultraviolet rays.

Be realistic about your body. Many people hold unrealistic ideals about what their body should look like. The shape and appearance of each body is dependent on many factors, including genes. Plastic surgery is a choice that increasing numbers of people make to achieve a body image they desire. But surgery carries with it many risks. Be well informed.

Donate a cat carrier to an animal shelter. The carriers come in handy when transporting cats, and animal rescue organizations are always looking for ones in good condition. Or you could give it to a cat owner you know who doesn't have the financial means to purchase one.

Mop the floor of a friend's flooded house. If a friend's house has suffered disaster-related damages, help her do the cleanup. Not only does a disaster like a flood pose an inconvenience to a homeowner or apartment dweller, it can be a devastating emotional experience.

Buy fresh fruits and vegetables in bulk. Not only will you be helping your family eat healthier and supporting local farmers, you'll also be saving some pennies. Packaging cost is carefully calculated into the price of the product. You didn't think you were getting it free, did you? Not only do you have to pay for it, but you also have to recycle or otherwise dispose of it.

Dust for someone with dust allergies.

Focus on seeing things for what they are. Develop the attitude that you must try to see things and people as they truly are, not as you wish them to be.

Build a support network. Stuck is the worst place to be, both physically and psychologically. Creating a network of friends that each of you can reach out to when times get rough ensures that you will all be able to carry on and move forward.

Give dark chocolate. Once in a while a piece of dark chocolate is just what is needed to lift a mood or satisfy a craving. Dark chocolate contains flavonoids, compounds with antioxidants that inhibit or slow down damage to the body by free radicals (unstable oxygen molecules that harm cell structures). So next time you buy someone a box of chocolates, go for dark chocolate.

Do not judge others. Try to understand them. It is much better to judge yourself and change what you do not like after a period of honest introspection.

Stimulate your brain. Remember this: boredom is bad for the brain. Give your and your friends' brains a workout. Try a few exercises like thinking of opposites and doing simple math as fast as possible. The best way to fight off dementia is by constantly working out your brain.

Don't spread your cold! Colds are caused by a family of more than two hundred different viruses. You can spread your cold by simply shaking someone's hand. If you have a cold, wash your hands frequently and cover your mouth with the crook of your arm (not your hand) when you cough.

Donate a first aid kit to a women's shelter.

Buckle up. Every time you get behind the wheel, make sure those you are driving put on their seatbelts. Wearing seatbelts saves lives. It could save yours and theirs.

Get interested in a friend's life. All too often, we tell others all about ourselves. In fact, most of us would rather the conversation be all about us most of the time. Resist the urge to make it be all about you. Take the time to really get to know someone else. Ask lots of questions.

Give gifts. Bombard the love of your life with tokens of affection and appreciation—from thoughtful notes (you later can put these in a scrapbook about your life together) to special evenings, intimate dinners, and pillow talk. Resist taking each other for granted, and celebrate your love.

Coach a children's sports team. If you don't know how to play the particular sport, volunteer to help the coach and do whatever is needed. Demonstrate good sportsmanship on the ball field, ice rink, or gymnastics floor.

Help your friend with her business. Encourage a friend in business for herself to charge more for her services and to set fees to get what her skills, expertise, and talents are truly worth.

Encourage a loved one to get help or counseling. Find a caring way to tell him that what he is doing is wrong and hurtful to himself and others. Set firm boundaries to protect yourself in the event that he turns his hostility on you.

Teach a child to cook. Make sure the project is age-appropriate and the child's safety is ensured. Make it fun and easy. Cooking together will instill confidence in the child and provide a way for you to spend quality time together.

Wash vegetables and fruits before serving them. Peel them, if possible, to keep from ingesting any harmful pesticides that they may have on them. Use a stiff brush to scrub root crops such as potatoes, parsnips, and turnips before cooking them. This will help to keep you and your loved ones healthy.

Use biodegradable bags. Pick up some earth-friendly bags the next time you're at PetCo or other pet stores. Choosing to clean up your pet's mess with something like BioBag—100% biodegradable dog waste bags—will help the environment and your neighborhood.

Stop being defensive. If you flip into a knee-jerk reaction and a defensive stance each time you hear something you don't agree with, understand that your body also undergoes assault due to rising levels of stress and anger. This diminishes your body's immune system.

Pack a first-aid kit for your family. Find out what goes into a home first-aid kit and put one together for your family. Your preparation could save someone from serious injury. Start by checking out the info on WebMD at *www.emedicine health.com/first_aid_kits/page5_em.htm*.

Raise awareness about spaying and neutering. Spaying and neutering animals reduces the growing populations of stray dogs and cats and can have an added benefit of reducing the incidents of humans being bitten by such animals infected with rabies or other diseases.

Write a love poem. Tell your lover how much he or she means to you in verse. Leave it on a pillow along with a chocolate and an I.O.U. for a massage when your schedules permit.

Help your parents stave off dementia. The best way to avoid age-related dementia is through learning. So, teach them how to play the violin, encourage them to learn a new language, or start playing mahjong or chess with them.

Create a going-away present as a family. Involve your entire family in making individual quilt squares to honor someone moving away. Each square could demonstrate some way that person was important in your life. Sew the squares together. Add a border and a backing.

Believe in second chances. Open yourself to infinite possibilities in relationships, love, and happiness. Second, third, and fourth chances do come around.

Encourage a friend to exercise and diet with you. Reinforce each other's efforts to get healthy and stay that way. Sometimes the hardest part of staying healthy is doing it alone.

Make a donation to an animal sterilization clinic. Look into organizations like Spay Neuter Assistance Program (SNAP) or the American Society for the Prevention of Cruelty to Animals (ASPCA). Through spay/neuter clinics on wheels, such organizations usually offer services free or at reduced fees to low-income families receiving public assistance such as Food Stamps. To find out more, go to *www.spayusa.org* or *www.aspca.org*.

Read to your children.

Change your furnace filters often. So often forgotten about, this chore will help ensure the air you and your family are breathing inside your house is healthful. When replacing a furnace, consider getting one that provides microfiltration. Indoor air in homes and offices can be more polluted than the outside air. People with allergies need a clean environment, and that includes improving air quality.

Give a massage. Nothing promotes the sense of healing and nurturing like the human touch. We all need it. So offer a massage to a friend. If you don't think you can give a good enough one, then pay for a massage. Many spas offer a variety of types, such as Japanese, Swedish, Ayurvedic, and myriad others. Some include aromatherapy and a hot pre-soak before the massage.

Pick a friend up at the airport. This is especially nice if her flight comes in late at night. She is likely to be exhausted and possibly not as alert as she would normally be to drive herself home or deal with hailing a taxi or catching a shuttle. Besides, having a friend or family member pick her up after a trip makes the last leg of the journey much more tolerable and much less stressful.

Inspire the love of theater in children. Establish a children's theater group in your community, either through a park and recreation department, a local school, or on your own with help from other parents. Involve the children in every aspect, from making costumes to painting sets and acting. It exposes them to potential career paths while encouraging teamwork and self-expression.

Aid in the rescue of parrots and parakeets. Dogs and cats aren't the only animals that need to be rescued. Make a donation to a bird-specific aid organization like Parrot Sanctuary. For more information, go to *www.parrotzoo.com* and make a donation.

Protect your pet during disasters. Develop a disaster preparedness plan and include options in that plan for your pets. The American Red Cross advocates acting to protect pets at the first sign of impending disaster. For more information, go to the American Red Cross website (*www.redcross.org*) and adapt a plan for pet protection.

Write a children's story about your kid. Whether it's an action adventure in which your child saves the day or a fairy tale where she lives happily ever after, she will be captivated by it and love that you took the time to write it. This is an especially good gift for a birthday.

Practice conscious eating. Mindless munching in front of the television can be a factor in weight gain. Think about each morsel before putting it into your mouth. Will it be good or bad for you? Also, understand that it takes about twenty minutes after you have eaten for the brain to signal the end of the urge to eat.

Give your cat natural catnip. You can grow the herb catnip in your garden for your cat. Cats like it but will not overdose on it. Dried, it can be stuffed into cat toys. Some sources assert that nepetalactone in catnip also repels mosquitoes, cockroaches, and some types of rodents. Check out *www .cat-world.com.au/Catnip.htm* for more information.

Volunteer to work at a local animal shelter. Let the organization know about any special skills or expertise you have, such as editing a newsletter, designing a radio/TV ad campaign, or brainstorming fundraising ideas. See *www.hsus .org* and learn how you can help the cause.

Help your family go paperless. Try to get important records, schedules, and calendars of school activities and family events onto the computer. The less paper you use as a household, the more you're helping the environment.

Buy your child a new toy for no reason.

Focus on seeing things for what they are. Develop the attitude that you must try to see things and people as they truly are, not as you wish them to be.

Go back to school. If you have longed to return to school after the kids were grown, go for it. Make it your personal goal to get that degree or advanced degree. It's never too late to do good for yourself, and your happiness at achieving your goal will affect everyone else around you.

Get your friends to kick their habit. Share the dangerous facts about smoking. Nicotine dependence is the number one chemical dependence in the United States. Nicotine is as addictive as cocaine, heroine, and alcohol. Smoking may cause premature death from heart disease, stroke, and cancer, and yet the tobacco companies aggressively market their products not only to rich countries but also to developing nations. Find out more about the harmful effects of smoking at *www.cdc.gov/tobacco/data_statistics*.

Break out of a rut as soon as you're in one. Try something new, whether or not you think you'll like it. The important part of shaking things up is that you gain knowledge about new products, new activities, new foods, etc. that you wouldn't if you remained in your rut. Change is good for your brain.

Stop name-calling people's body parts. Have you joked about your "ten-gallon neck," his "unibrow," or her "thunder thighs"? If so, stop and appreciate the gift of the human body. If someone's body is healthy and getting him through each day with very few problems, then why make fun? Replace those negative epithets with positive attributions and affirmations.

Bring the joy of animals to at-risk youth. Volunteer to work with an organization that offers the healing touch of animals to those children and teens who need it the most. Check out programs like those run through the Gentle Barn (*www .gentlebarn.org*).

Think positively. When you imagine wonderful things in your life, imagine equally
wonderful things manifesting in the lives of
others.

Invite your partner out for a wild afternoon. Take him or her to the zoo. Learn about the animals and make a donation to support their care and feeding.

Promote healthy living. Make sure your family is not only eating and exercising well, but is also in a good state of mental health. Talk to them. Cheer them up. Get them to discuss their feelings. This is especially important for pregnant women, because in caring for their bodies and minds, they are directly affecting their unborn child.

Offer to help with a friend's wedding. It can be overwhelming, and an extra pair of hands and eyes may be just what the family needs. Whether it's running simple errands or helping set up the event hall, you'll be a big help to the bride-to-be.

Start a book club and discussion group. A book club is a great way for people to share their love of reading, build a sense of community, and express their ideas in an open forum.

Be there to do the small things on moving day. Moving day is a hectic time, so be there for your friend. Offer to do a run to a local coffee shop; she probably doesn't have the time to make a pot of java. Provide encouraging words, as she may be feeling a little overwhelmed. Help her focus on what needs to be done, be there at the end to support her, and know that strong friendships can be sustained across many miles and over lifetimes.

Compliment your partner's inner beauty. Appreciate his or her kindness, grace, intelligence, humor, and generosity—all sexy and sought-after attributes that are far better and longer-lasting than an expensive facial, manicure, and hair-cut. Inner beauty is more attractive and longer-lasting than physical appearance.

Remain positive. Don't be a self-defeatist. Accept that you are someone unique (because you are). There is no one else exactly like you in the world; even identical twins or multiples have some differences. Celebrate your gifts and talents. Focus on them rather than on what you lack. You are here for a reason.

Adopt a child who's lost his parents. Permanent adoptive families are needed to care for children who have been neglected, abused, and even abandoned. See what help you might offer to ease the heartbreak these parentless children experience waiting for someone to love them. Go to *www .childrenawaitingparents.com.*

Know when *not* to involve yourself. Recognize when someone in crisis does *not* want your help, and respect her position. It is one of the hardest things to do. Our impulse is to rush in and fix the problem. But we have to remember it is her crisis, not ours. We must honor her desire to figure things out alone.

Do a friend's dishes. Clear and do the dishes the next time you have dinner at the home of a friend, neighbor, or acquaintance. It shows good manners and is a great way to thank her for having you over.

Do something new with your partner. Psychologists say sharing novel experiences can deepen your happiness.

Take the whole family on a weekend outing. A short trip to a local strawberry patch in the summer or an apple orchard in the fall can be fun for the kids and relaxing for the parents. When the entire family participates in frequent outings, it brings everyone closer together and reduces the tensions that have built up during the week.

Don't worry. Does worry help? Probably not, so why do it? Replace worry with positive affirmations and a strong and clear mental image of what you want in your life. Use your will, yoked with a positive course of action, to make it happen.

Keep children and teens busy with fun activities. Volunteer at after-school clubs, summer camps, church events, and service projects. A youngster with too much time and nothing to do is more likely to get into trouble than a child who has an active social life.

Donate used household electronics to charities. Box up old fax machines, monitors, computers, televisions, radios, and cell phones that your family no longer uses to donate to worthwhile causes. They are always looking for functioning equipment that is in good shape.

Take care of your skin. If it is dry and cracked, fill a tub full of warm water and pour in a few capfuls of body oil. Get into the tub and lie on your back, then stomach, then back again. Massage the oil into your skin. When you get out of the tub, take care not to slip. Continue rubbing in the oil all over, and then pat your skin dry. The fine lines and cracks will have disappeared.

Knit something for a new addition. If you've recently added a new member to your immediate or extended family, make some booties, a sweater, or a hat for the new baby. These types of personally crafted gifts truly come from the heart and will be appreciated and cherished by the parents.

Don't let your friend drive drunk. Call a taxi for him if he's had too much alcohol. Ensure your friend's safety. Drive him home yourself or find another means of safe transportation for him. A taxi ride is generally a safe way to travel, but a person who is inebriated necessarily places her trust in the driver, a total stranger. If you are the designated driver, take your friend home. If you are not driving, then ride with him in the taxi. Only then can you be completely sure that he has made it home safely.

Take a class and learn about conflict resolution. Apply it to the relationships in your life, and watch how the causes of conflicts begin to shift or diminish.

Protect your child from abduction. Teach her how to handle unwanted advances, especially from strangers. The Polly Klass Foundation and other such organizations work to educate people on how to avoid abductions and help find missing children. See *www.pollyklaas.org*.

Swap skills with a friend. Offer to teach a friend how to make killer guacamole or a chocolate soufflé in exchange for showing you how to change a tire, check your car's engine oil level, or change the spark plugs. You both benefit from sharing your knowledge with each other.

Strive for equality in your love relationship. Relationships in which the couples share equally in sacrifices, decision-making, communication, and chores are more likely to succeed than those relationships in which one person dominates the other.

Help a friend who wants to learn to cook. Buy him new pans or donate some of your old ones, and while you are at it, throw in one of your cookbooks. Don't do it because he might reward you with a gourmet meal sometime in the future; do it because it will give him such joy to have the necessary tools to start cooking.

Plan a children's tea party. Invite bears, dolls, and other stuffed animals. Use a special pot, like a lily pad–shaped pot with a frog lid, and institute silly rules like everyone must wear hats. Allow the children to set the table with napkins, spoons, and teacups (espresso cups are just the right size for small hands). Add a plate of sandwiches and a jar of gingersnaps. The children will love it.

Plant some perennials in a cancer patient's garden. Put them where he can see them blooming. Annuals die each year and must be replaced, but perennials return year after year. Your gesture is a small, unspoken statement of your hope.

221

Boycott unregulated foreign products. In particular, do not support products coming from places where governments exploit their own people, force people to work in unsafe conditions, and sustain control of power through threats of violence or imprisonment.

Find the greater good in every moment. Learn from the stressful and negative experiences, but put your energy into finding the silver lining, seeing the good, and praising it.

Carry a piece of luggage for a stranger. Help an elderly person or mom with a stroller carry large pieces of luggage. Chances are they have been toting those big bags around for a while now and could use the help.

Expand your horizons. Take a lifelong learning trip offered through a university. You can go on an archaeological dig, an Audubon expedition, a history excursion, or myriad other adventures, often with a college professor as your guide and guest lecturer. Learning more about the world you live in will make you a better person.

Truly listen to your partner's joys and concerns. Take time out to listen, even just about the events of the day. Make sure you're actually listening and not interrupting with your own stories.

Let someone have the taxi you've just hailed. Next time you hail a cab while it's busy on the street, let the person standing next to you have it. This simple gesture may cost a few minutes of your time, but it will mean the world to the stranger you helped.

Allow someone to go out in front of you from the elevator. Don't rush in front of people the next time to you go to exit an elevator. Let the other occupants get out before you go on with your day.

Be a foster parent. Provide a stable, safe, nurturing, temporary home for a child who has been abandoned. Families are needed to care for children who, through no fault of their own, have ended up in these unfortunate situations.

Help a child learn about investing. Start with the financial basics: earning, saving, and finding ways to make the money grow. What better way to help a young person develop some real-world skills that will serve him throughout life?

Pay for the person behind you. Next time you pull up to the drive-thru window, pay for what you ordered *and* what the person behind you ordered. When it's his turn to pay, he'll be pleasantly surprised by your kind act.

Write your lover a love letter. Fill it with your thoughts of a strong and deep inner passion, and make it long. (A succinctly written love letter, according to twentieth-century English politician Duff Cooper, is a bit too much like lightning.)

Hold the elevator door for someone.

Help a friend with her yard sale. Having items already sorted, in labeled boxes, and marked with prices on stickers or tags makes it easier to move the merchandise because buyers don't have to ask the prices.

Make a dream come true for an ill child. Become a volunteer at your local chapter of Dream Factory, an organization that works with volunteers, nonprofit organizations, and corporations to procure dreams for children who suffer from a life-threatening illness. Find out more about the organization at *www.dreamfactoryinc.com*.

Keep your friend's glass half full. Be an optimist and try to help her see the "best-case scenario" rather than its opposite. Whether it is love, health, finances, or a job issue that she's worrying about, help her let it go, relax, and let in the good.

Open a door for someone carrying packages. Lend an extra hand to someone who needs it. If you see someone juggling a bunch of packages, go grab the door for them. This little extra effort will help prevent any tumbling and breaking.

Return lost items. Don't just assume someone else will do it. Immediately return a found wallet, money, or other item that someone has dropped or left behind. Your decision to help out could have a huge impact on someone else's life.

Be thankful for the gift of your life. It's nothing short of miraculous to be in the world. We are equipped with special talents and gifts to help us in life. These are the best kinds of possessions, ones for which we ought to be grateful.

Give up your seat on a bus. Whether it's to an elderly person, a pregnant woman, a young mother with several children, a physically challenged person, or someone who just looks weary, giving your seat up will help that person out and brighten his or her day.

Help someone out at the grocery store. Reach high to retrieve a grocery item for someone who wants it but can't reach it. If neither of you can reach it, offer to summon help.

Be punctual. Don't make your friends wait. Show them that you respect their time. When you agree to meet for socializing, don't be late. Chronic lateness suggests many negatives: you don't care, you don't know how to budget time, you are a procrastinator, or you are careless and do not pay attention to details (like knowing what time it is).

Don't talk about stress; do something about it. Break the cycle of complaining about your high stress level. That's just expending mental energy to bring more stress your way. Instead, focus on how you can de-stress your life.

Balance unkindness with acts of kindness. If the person in the line ahead of you at the bank snaps rudely at the teller, shift the energy. When it is your turn, say something to lift her spirits.

Pay back any money that you owe, whether to a family member, a friend, or a business colleague. Make the effort to do the right thing, even if you can afford to make only small payments.

Stop being competitive. Let go of competition with your lover or spouse over who earns the most money. In the grand scheme of things, it really doesn't matter, does it? Just count your blessings that you both can contribute to your income.

Help someone change a flat tire, even if it's raining. If you've ever had to change a flat tire on your own before, you know how much of a hassle it can be. So next time you see someone changing a tire on the side of the road, pull over and offer an extra hand—even if it's just to hold an umbrella over his head.

Pull all the way forward at the gas pump. This way the car following can use the pump behind you. Otherwise, that driver will have to wait until you finish pumping your gas, find another pump, or do some tricky maneuvering to get into a position elsewhere at the station.

Over-tip a good waiter or waitress.

Forgive. Priests, psychologists, and medical doctors know that the act of forgiveness helps heal a person's body as well as heart, mind, and soul. You may think forgiving helps the other person, but, in fact, it helps you.

Keep a secret. When a friend, relative, child, or business associate tells you something in confidence, do your utmost to honor them by keeping their secret.

Be sincere. When asked a question, tell the truth. Be brave enough to speak openly from your heart to your friends when they seek your opinion. Don't be duplicitous, saying one thing to their face and something different behind their back. Your friends will appreciate your sincerity, and you will begin to feel honor-bound to tell the truth.

Empty your pantry for a young relative's first house. Buying a home is a big step. Filling the kitchen cupboards with food is an additional expense at a time when it may seem to them that the cash register has been constantly ringing. Help a young relative by filling his cupboards for him.

Allow your friends to pay you back in other ways. If a friend is strapped for cash and you have lent him some money, let him do something for you rather than actually *paying* you back. Instead of giving you money, he could clean your house, wash windows, mow the lawn, or cook a meal.

Take a break from fast food. Reacquaint yourself, your family, and friends with the pleasure of taking time to prepare a great meal from the freshest and highest-quality ingredients. You'll be giving yourself a gift as well as others.

Be a true friend. Don't be someone who uses friends to constantly complain, spread gossip, or backstab others. Friendships won't last if bathed in an environment of resentment, anger, or self-pity. Don't neglect your friendships. There's truth in the old expression, "To have a friend, you must be a friend."

Speak kindly. If people around you are complaining about life, listen compassionately to their complaints and acknowledge the suffering they are feeling, but don't feed it.

Keep your promises. Follow through whenever you give your word. If you make a promise to someone and then forget about it ten minutes later, that failure to follow through violates any trust you may have established. Remember what you promised to do and then do it.

Speak out against hateful comments. When you hear racial slurs or epithets hurled at someone, stand up for them. Refuse to be complicit in the act by your inaction. Call law enforcement if the person is threatened or the situation deteriorates. Do something. Apathy is bad karma.

Handle conflicts without negative confrontations. Find new words that are neutral, as opposed to inflammatory language, to clearly and precisely express difficult feelings toward loved ones, business associates, or coworkers. Avoid bringing up past conversations, situations, or events that might trigger a defensive, hostile, or aggressive act toward you. Try to remain calm even as you explain the problem and endeavor to establish boundaries for self-preservation. Doing something good for yourself, like establishing limits or boundaries, is of primary importance.

Admit when you're wrong. Go to the person involved and apologize. It will make them feel validated, and you will generate good karma as you learn from your mistake.

Have your friends buy local produce. Get them together for a weekend of picking fruit from local orchards. When you've plucked all the bounty from the trees, take a few boxes or bags of the fruit to a local food bank or homeless shelter.

Send a care package to your child in college. When your college-age daughter becomes frustrated, hopeless, or a little depressed during her final examinations, make her a special basket. Put in scented oils, French-milled soaps, mint lotion for the feet, pumice, nail clippers, a bag of chamomile tea, and a CD of beautiful or relaxing music.

Give the gift of separation. Allow for some time apart from your partner to appreciate your relationship. Love depends more on the quality of time spent together than on the amount of time. Time apart can be healthy and good for a romantic relationship.

Become a Big Brother or Big Sister volunteer. Your commitment could have a positive impact on the life of a young person. For example, more than half of the kids with a Big Brother or Big Sister are less inclined to ditch school, and roughly forty-six percent steer clear of using illegal substances. Visit *www.bbbs.org* for more information.

Invite a neighbor's children to the movies with yours. It'll heighten your youngsters' enjoyment of their afternoon outing. Although your neighbor may reciprocate—ensuring your own child-free afternoon—don't expect or count on it. Do your good deed and know that you made it possible for a group of kids to have a wonderful day.

Remember single friends during special times. Keep your friend who is single and without family in mind on his birthday and at other holiday times during the year. Invite him to celebratory dinners, send him birthday greetings (even if it is just an e-mail card), and introduce him to your other single friends. Your efforts of inclusion might mean his support network will grow.

Make sure your mother and aunts get regular mammograms. Early detection of breast cancer saves lives. See *www.center4research.org* for more information.

Make chicken soup for an ill family member. It soothes sore throats in people with colds and the flu and its anti-inflammatory agents may even boost the immune system.

Be responsible about your finances. Try not to spend money you don't have. Keep track of your credit card debt and pay off the entire bill, if you can, every billing cycle.

Help fix up a friend's home before she sells it. You might pack boxes, wrap pictures and paintings in brown paper for shipping, put outdated documents through a shredder so they don't have to be part of the move, clean out the garage so excess furniture can be put there when the new carpet goes in, or go through the house with spackle and a trowel to patch small nail holes in preparation for the painters. A move is a huge transition for most of us. The help of friends is invaluable during that time.

Cook a meal for a relative with a new baby. After the birth of a baby, everyone's so busy there's hardly any time to eat. Help out the family by putting together a homemade dinner and delivering it to their home.

Reward yourself. Every time you hit a milestone in a big project, give yourself a treat. Sometimes just knowing there's a little reward waiting is enough of an impetus to keep you on track.

Return kind gestures. If a friend brings you a basket of bounty from her yard or a plate with a homemade treat, respond in kind. When the basket or plate is empty, put fruit or vegetables in the basket and cookies or a slice of homemade pie or cake on the plate before returning the basket or dish to its owner.